Southern Living

comfort food

a delicious trip down memory lane

©2009 by Oxmoor House, Inc.
Book Division of Southern Progress Corporation
P. O. Box 2262, Birmingham, Alabama 35201-2262

Southern Living is a federally registered trademark belonging to Southern Living, Inc.

ISBN-13: 978-0-8487-3266-0
ISBN-10: 0-8487-3266-9
Library of Congress Control Number: 2008930048

Printed in the United States of America
Second Printing 2009

Foreword ©2009 by Pat Conroy

Oxmoor House, Inc.
Editor in Chief: Nancy Fitzpatrick Wyatt
Executive Editor: Susan Payne Dobbs
Art Director: Keith McPherson
Managing Editor: Allison Long Lowery

Southern Living **Comfort Food**
Editor: Julie Gunter
Project Editor: Diane Rose
Senior Designer: Melissa Jones Clark
Copy Chief: L. Amanda Owens
Director, Test Kitchens: Elizabeth Tyler Austin
Assistant Director, Test Kitchens: Julie Christopher
Test Kitchens Professionals: Jane Chambliss, Patricia Michaud, Kathleen Royal Phillips,
    Catherine Crowell Steele, Ashley T. Strickland, Deborah Wise
Photography Director: Jim Bathie
Senior Photo Stylist: Kay E. Clarke
Associate Photo Stylist: Katherine Eckert Coyne
Director of Production: Laura Lockhart
Senior Production Manager: Greg A. Amason

Contributors
Composite: Carol O. Loria
Editorial Contributor: Rebecca R. Benton
Proofreader: Carmine B. Loper
Indexer: Mary Ann Laurens
Interns: Anne-Harris Jones, Shea Staskowski, Lauren Wiygul
Food Stylists: Margaret Dickey, Ana Price Kelly, Debby Maugans
Photographers: Tina Cornett, Jennifer Davick, Will Dickey, Beau Gustafson, Lee Harrelson,
    Beth Dreiling Hontzas, Art Meripol, Mark Sandlin, Karim Shamsi-Basha, Amy Jo Young
Photo Stylists: Mindi Shapiro Levine, Leslie Simpson

To order additional publications, call 1-800-765-6400.

For more books to enrich your life, visit **oxmoorhouse.com**

To search, savor, and share thousands of recipes, visit **myrecipes.com**

Cover: Classic Strawberry Shortcake (page 211), Three-Cheese Pasta Bake (page 13)
Back Cover: Lemon Meringue Pie (page 207), Gonzales Meat Loaf (page 16), Million-Dollar Pound Cake (page 185)

{ contents }

❈ { foreword } ❈

Comfort food is something my family lived without, but I think we would have really liked it if our mother had served it at mealtime. In other places I have written about my mother's lamentable qualities as a cook. My maternal grandmother, Stanny, was even worse, and I'd want to run from the kitchen when I found her preparing a meal. She made biscuits so hard you could kill squirrels with them after dinner. But Stanny would always electrify me with news of her world travels, using phrases like, "I ate python in Tanganyika." I remember thinking, "Well, I sure hope you didn't cook it, Stanny."

I recall an argument between my grandmother and mother as to who was the worse cook, and they both made good cases for themselves. To me, my grandmother was the most incompetent cook ever to walk into a Southern kitchen. She wore that fact like a badge of honor. Whenever Stanny made a batch of cornbread, it tasted like neither corn nor bread, but a runny gruel you could eat like a soup if you were so inclined. On the day of the argument, Stanny and my mother imported some mountain wisdom when they said, matter-of-factly, that it hadn't been necessary for either of them to learn to cook because both had been born beautiful. As they saw it, they had to perfect the art of "dolling up" in order to attract men, but they couldn't risk their manicures by moving heavy pots and pans around a kitchen.

My wife, the novelist Cassandra King, can drive me to the point of lunacy by recalling the comfort food that her mother, Pat King, provided her three daughters during their growing up on a peanut farm in south Alabama. In a dreamy voice, Cassandra recites endless litanies of cakes and pies that her mother would make from scratch. They had dessert every day of her life. She licks her lips when she describes her mother's lemon meringue or pecan pies baking in the oven, or the time her mother would put into the patient assembly of an old-fashioned pound cake, or her coconut cake that was always made with freshly grated coconut. Then my wife switches to the main meal,

Comfort food, at least in my mind, should be some ambrosial pleasure that comes out of your childhood.

where the chicken was fried to perfection, the bass taken from the ponds on the farm, and the roasts surrounded by vegetables they had grown in their own garden. The vegetables were next: the new butterbeans, field peas, turnip greens, and the tomatoes red and glistening, picked that morning with dew still on them. I've listened to these stories so many times I've always wondered why the King sisters didn't weigh three hundred pounds by the time they got to high school.

Cassandra is an excellent cook herself, but she hands the baton of best cook directly to her mother. Unlike mine, her childhood was a well-fed and happy one.

As I sat down to write on the subject of the comfort food in my life for this book, I thought the editors of Oxmoor House had made the worst decision about the person to write this essay. Comfort food, at least in my mind, should be some ambrosial pleasure that comes out of your childhood. Though I love to write about food, I didn't know much about it until I escaped my mother's ghastly table. In something of a panic, I called my brothers and sisters. I could not come up with a single example of comfort food that our mother provided us with, either on a regular or irregular basis. Was I exaggerating, or did I have it all wrong?

"Comfort food?" my brother Mike said. "What's that?"

"Something you looked forward to eating, even if it was a guilty pleasure," I explained.

"Comfort foods?" Mike scoffed. "We didn't have any. Wait a minute—a glass of milk and a box of vanilla wafers."

"Okay," I agreed, "that's a comfort food. But not a very good one."

"The best I got," Mike said.

My brother Jim was the only champion of our mother's cooking I could find among the children. From the beginning of our conversation, Jim rhapsodized about Mom's meat loaf, which the rest of us thought tasted like one of Dad's lace-up shoes.

"Her meat loaf was dry as dirt," I argued.

"It was perfect," Jim said. "I would select meat loaf as my favorite of her comfort foods, but it wasn't her specialty. She made the best biscuits I ever ate, and she made them from a secret family recipe."

"We don't have any secret family recipes," I said. "And I don't even remember Mom making us biscuits."

"She took that secret recipe with her to her grave," Jim told me.

"What a loss to cuisine," I said.

The Sunday following my conversations with Mike and Jim, my sister Kathy drove out to our house on Fripp Island with my nephew, Willie, the only musician my family has ever produced. Willie takes an abnormal pleasure in his uncles' whining and cursing the forces of darkness as we tell the stories of our ridiculous childhood. My sister actually laughed out loud when I asked about comfort food in our mother's house.

... Stanny and my mother imported some mountain wisdom when they said, matter-of-factly, that it hadn't been necessary for either of them to learn to cook because both had been born beautiful.

"Our mother couldn't cook," Kathy said. "How could she make anyone comfort food?"

"Is Uncle Pat going to be writing more lies about our family, Mama?" Willie said. He does it to irritate me.

"The man's got to make a living," my sister explained. "Let's go over the dinners of our childhood, Pat, and maybe we can figure out something."

"Shoot," I said.

"You were a boy and may not have noticed this, but we ate certain things every day of the week. And it was the same each week. On Mondays, we had Morton's chicken pot pies," she said.

"That's why I hate chicken pot pies to this day. I get nauseated if I smell one cooking."

"Our brother Mike still loves them," Kathy told me. "He's got a freezer full of them."

"Tuesdays?" I asked.

"Meat loaf with canned green beans," Kathy replied. "On Wednesday, we had frozen macaroni and cheese. We had iceberg lettuce with French dressing on it. On Thursdays, it was hamburgers. But never with buns."

"You were a boy and may not have noticed this, but we ate certain things every day of the week."

"Don't even speak about Friday," I said.

"Frozen fish sticks," Kathy said in triumph as Willie made gagging noises. "And Brother Mike keeps a bunch of fish sticks in his freezer, too, next to the pot pies. If he were truthful, he would tell you that fish sticks are still a comfort food to him."

"Jim bragged about Mom's biscuits," I told her. "Claims she made them with a secret family recipe."

"Nonsense," Kathy laughed. "Don't you remember the swing and the bump on the counter?" She pantomimed a chopping motion with her arm.

Suddenly a sound from my childhood, an accurate thud, came back to me. I recalled seeing my young mother swinging a cylinder of Pillsbury refrigerated biscuits with enough force to split the cardboard. The factory-made biscuits would spill out over the counter, and Mom would scoop them up and line them in a pan. So much for Brother Jim's memory of scrumptious and comforting bread made from a recipe handed down for generations by the secrecy-addicted females of my family. In the recounting of our family's culinary history, Jim found

I recalled seeing my young mother swinging a cylinder of Pillsbury refrigerated biscuits with enough force to split the cardboard.

himself discredited and mocked, especially in his zeal for Mom's tasteless meat loaf.

I asked Kathy about desserts. "I remember eating cakes," I told her.

"Very rarely, and then out of cake boxes. Never from scratch," she replied. "Do you remember what happened if you stole a piece of cake?"

"Mom would go ballistic."

"But we learned to cut it left-handed when we stole a piece," Kathy said. "That way, Mom would always blame Dad."

"Those cakes were terrible," I said.

"Not as bad as her spaghetti, though," Kathy said. "Sunday was Italian night, remember?"

"The worst night of the week," I recalled. "What would she do to the pasta?"

"Cook it for a very long time," said my sister. "Then when she dumped it into the colander it was a solid lump, stuck together in a gooey ball."

"Then there was her ghastly meat sauce."

"She'd cook up some hamburger meat, then throw in a can or two of tomato sauce. That's what she spooned over the wad of spaghetti and called spaghetti sauce."

"Italian night," I sighed. "I didn't know I loved pasta until I moved to Italy."

When I talked to my youngest brother, Tim, he had the darkest and most troubled memories about the dinners of our childhood. Without equivocation, he declared that the evening meal was the most terrifying time of the day for him.

"My favorite comfort food?" Tim said. "A knuckle sandwich. No, let me be clear about this. There was never any comfort food. None. For us to get comfort food, someone had to die in Alabama."

Whenever one of our relatives died in Piedmont, Alabama, the Conroy children rejoiced. We did so because of the meal after the funeral service, where we filled our plates with many things, among them fried chicken and thick slices of golden ham. At one of those funerals, I ate potato salad for the first time, a creamy coleslaw, fried catfish, perfectly seasoned beans of all description, and fresh corn on the cob, which my Uncle Russ had to teach me how to eat. The dessert table was nothing short of magnificent, with its glistening

As my father told stories, I cooked for him in the kitchen.... I could let my father see how much I had come to love him by serving him and his visitors comfort food.

fruit pies, tall lemon meringues, beautifully shaped cakes of every variety—all of them made from scratch. I learned the term "made from scratch" at the first funeral I attended in Piedmont.

At the last funeral I attended in Piedmont several years ago, they buried my beloved Uncle Cicero. I tried to watch the proceedings with adult eyes. I went back into the kitchen where the women were getting the food ready for the coming feast, and before they shooed me out of there, I could see the intense labor that those aunts and cousins were putting into the preparation of this massive meal. My aunt Ruby Kiser was the ringleader as she marshaled all the feminine energy into a well-ordered army that was about to feed the mourners of a deeply beloved man. As I watched these women carrying plates and dishes out to the tables groaning under the weight of this seemingly endless bounty, I could see clearly what essence my mother and grandmother had missed during their growing up. They had failed to recognize that comfort food, well-prepared food of any kind, is a secret but articulate language. It is a way of telling families how important they are to them, and how much they want them to be happy. But its deepest expression is a wordless and foolproof way of letting our families know the profound depth of our love for them. Comfort food says I love you without saying a single word.

When my father was dying of cancer, his friends and family came out regularly to eat dinner at my home. Some weeks, I would average twenty guests a night. I plied my father and his guests with shrimp and grits, crab cakes, oxtail and lamb shanks, endless pasta dishes, homemade ice cream, mashed potatoes with garlic, fried chicken, and vegetables from Barefoot Bubba's farm down the road. As my father told stories, I cooked for him in the kitchen. Though we had a terrible father-son relationship during my childhood, I could let my father see how much I had come to love him by serving him and his visitors comfort food. I wish I had had this cookbook with me that summer before my father died.

—Pat Conroy

She-Crab Soup

Here's a favorite comfort soup from the kitchen of Cassandra King and Pat Conroy.

Sherry
1   pound crabmeat
6   tablespoons butter
2   tablespoons grated onion
4   heaping tablespoons all-purpose flour
3   cups milk
2   chicken bouillon cubes
1   teaspoon salt
2   cups half-and-half or whipping cream
Chopped fresh parsley

While preparing other ingredients, pour some sherry over crabmeat to soak.

Melt butter in a deep soup pot. As butter's melting, grate 2 tablespoons onion into pot. (Important step—not chopped or minced—grated only!)

Make a white sauce by stirring flour into butter/onion and gradually adding 3 cups of milk.

When good and hot (the sauce, not you), add bouillon cubes (or equivalent granules) and salt. Once dissolved, add crabmeat, put a lid over it, and cook a minute or so. (Don't boil; simmer gently.)

Add 2 cups half-and-half (or cream, if you like it richer) and heat thoroughly. Top with a handful of chopped fresh parsley.

Serve steaming hot, and either pass around a cruet of sherry or drizzle it over the top.

Yield: 4 generous servings.

See page 288 for Pat Conroy's Pumpkin Pie.

comfort food classics

The Secret Ingredient

As I thumbed through my mother's *Auburn Cookbook,* I found more than a good cookie recipe. There was a note stuck to a page with a straight pin. It read, "I used this Standard Cookie recipe for Christmas cookies in 1982. Adam helped."

My 30-year-old son, Adam, was 4 at the time the note was written. Mama didn't leave behind a diary, but as I took a closer look at the cookbook, I found a scrapbook of memories of her life, illustrated in notes, recipes, and stains on the pages.

The inscription read, "To Pearl, From Mrs. Britton 1957." This book was a gift to my mother from her mother-in-law—and a timely one, too. I would have been 4 years old myself and in constant need of food in mass quantities. I was in good hands.

"Everything in moderation," Mama said when it came to food. But Daddy and I both urged excess when it came to the pies, cookies, and cakes she conjured. I found her recipe for piecrust on one dog-eared page, and her pastry really did flake with a fork, just like they used to show on TV.

On the front cover she taped a chocolate chip cookie recipe—the one Daddy and I clamored for often. Inside the cookbook cover was a yellowed clipping from *The Birmingham News* with a recipe for Red Velvet Cake, my birthday favorite when I was a teenager.

Buttermilk Pie, Pineapple Pride Cake, Baked Chicken Casserole—these were taken from magazines and stuck inside the book. Favorite recipes got a "good" written beside them, like Fudge Cake and Betty Crocker One Bowl Cake. Mama didn't use a lot of words. She used her hands.

A puzzling index card listed the ingredients for "Punch for 50." She did not like

continued

crowds much. Our family was small, and her compact kitchen was the center of her tiny kingdom. Mama had dinner on the table every night at the exact moment Daddy pulled into the garage at 5:30. I remember him opening the kitchen door, announcing, "I smell fried chicken," his face as alight as the brightest Christmas tree.

Her favorite newspaper column, "Hints From Heloise," was well represented, too, with a recipe for pralines. She'd say we had to have a dry day for candymaking. She always made fudge, divinity, and pralines for Christmas, a once-a-year extravagance.

Her practical side showed throughout the pages. A handwritten note inside the back cover explained how to prevent a weeping meringue. On the back of the cookbook, a household hint from Heloise told how to repair curtains. Mama made do. She knew how to stretch a pound of hamburger seven different ways and could cut up a chicken to make three meals from it. As a young woman working in a South Alabama bank during the Depression, she saw people lose their homes. Home meant everything, and food fueled the home.

Lots of love was the real secret ingredient in my mother's cooking. She found comfort showing her feelings in this way. I used to think her kitchen wizardry was an inborn gift. But in this book of happy memories, I saw by the splatters, the notes, and the well-worn pages that she had a guide to help show her the way.

Thankfully and gratefully, so did I.

—Wanda McKinney, Associate Travel Editor

Three-Cheese Pasta Bake

prep: 20 min. cook: 7 min. bake: 15 min.

Mac and cheese, the quintessential comfort food, gets a great update with penne pasta and a trio of cheeses.

1 (8-ounce) package penne pasta
2 tablespoons butter
2 tablespoons all-purpose flour
1½ cups milk
½ cup half-and-half
1 cup (4 ounces) shredded white Cheddar cheese
¼ cup grated Parmesan cheese
2 cups (8 ounces) shredded Gruyère cheese, divided
1 teaspoon salt
¼ teaspoon pepper
Pinch of ground nutmeg

Preheat oven to 350°. Prepare pasta according to package directions.

Meanwhile, melt butter in a saucepan over medium heat. Whisk in flour until smooth; cook, whisking constantly, 1 minute. Gradually whisk in milk and half-and-half; cook, whisking constantly, 3 to 5 minutes or until thickened. Stir in Cheddar cheese, Parmesan cheese, 1 cup Gruyère cheese, and next 3 ingredients until smooth.

Stir together pasta and cheese mixture; pour into a lightly greased 11- x 7-inch baking dish. Top with remaining 1 cup Gruyère cheese.

Bake, uncovered, at 350° for 15 minutes or until golden and bubbly. **Yield: 4 servings.**

Note: To make ahead, proceed with recipe as directed, but don't top with remaining 1 cup Gruyère cheese. Cover and chill up to 8 hours. Let stand at room temperature 30 minutes. Bake at 350° for 20 to 25 minutes or until bubbly. Increase oven temperature to 400°. Top with remaining Gruyère; bake 10 more minutes or until golden.

Barbecue Deviled Eggs

prep: 30 min.   cook: 6 min.   stand: 15 min.

Chopped barbecued pork is the filling's secret ingredient in this old-fashioned Southern favorite. If you want to omit the chopped pork, add a drop of liquid smoke to provide a barbecue-like flavor.

12   large eggs
¼   cup mayonnaise
1   tablespoon Dijon mustard
¼   teaspoon salt
½   teaspoon pepper
⅛   teaspoon hot sauce
⅓   cup finely chopped barbecued pork
      (without sauce)
Garnishes: paprika, chopped dill pickle

Place eggs in a single layer in a large saucepan; add water to a depth of 3 inches. Bring to a boil; cover, remove from heat, and let stand 15 minutes.

Drain and fill pan with cold water and ice. Tap each egg firmly on counter until cracks form all over shell. Peel under cold running water.

Cut eggs in half lengthwise, and carefully remove yolks. Mash yolks with mayonnaise. Stir in mustard and next 3 ingredients; blend well. Gently stir in pork.

Spoon yolk mixture into egg white halves. Chill until ready to serve. Garnish, if desired.

Yield: 12 servings.

Gonzales Meat Loaf

prep: 15 min.   bake: 1 hr., 10 min.   stand: 10 min.

Cilantro, brown sugar, and a heavy shake of hot sauce make this meat loaf well seasoned. As expected, leftovers make a great sandwich.

2   pounds ground sirloin
3   large eggs, lightly beaten
1   cup fine, dry breadcrumbs
4   garlic cloves, minced
1   medium-size red onion, chopped
2   plum tomatoes, seeded and chopped
1½   cups (6 ounces) shredded Monterey Jack cheese
¼   to ½ cup firmly packed brown sugar
½   cup chopped fresh cilantro
¼   cup Worcestershire sauce
2   tablespoons hot sauce
2   teaspoons salt
1   teaspoon pepper

Preheat oven to 350°. Combine all ingredients. Shape into a free-form 9- x 5-inch loaf, and place on a lightly greased rack in a broiler pan. **Bake** at 350° for 45 minutes; increase oven temperature to 425°, and bake 15 to 25 more minutes or until done. Let meat loaf stand 10 minutes before serving. **Yield: 6 to 8 servings.**

Home-Cooked Pole Beans

prep: 26 min.   cook: 19 min.

Here's an easy bean dish flavored with bacon drippings.

2   pounds fresh pole beans
3   bacon slices
1   teaspoon salt
½   teaspoon pepper
¼   teaspoon sugar

Wash beans; trim stem ends. Cut beans into 1½-inch pieces, and set aside.

Cook bacon in a large saucepan until crisp; remove bacon, reserving drippings in pan. Crumble bacon, and set aside.
Add 1 cup water and remaining 3 ingredients to saucepan; bring to a boil over high heat. Add beans; cover, reduce heat to medium, and cook 15 minutes or to desired doneness. Sprinkle with crumbled bacon. Serve with a slotted spoon. **Yield: 8 servings.**

Buttermilk-Garlic Mashed Potatoes

prep: 10 min.   cook: 6 min.

2   tablespoons butter
3   garlic cloves, chopped
2   cups buttermilk
⅔   cup milk
½   teaspoon salt
½   teaspoon pepper
1   (22-ounce) package frozen mashed potatoes*

Melt butter in a Dutch oven over medium heat; add garlic, and sauté 1 minute.

Add buttermilk and next 3 ingredients. Cook, stirring constantly, 5 minutes or until thoroughly heated. Stir in potatoes until smooth. **Yield: 4 servings.**

*For testing purposes only, we used Ore-Ida Mashed Potatoes. There's no need to thaw them.

Beef Stroganoff

prep: 16 min.   cook: 41 min.

A universal homey entrée, this stroganoff turns out a big yield with plenty of gravy for sopping.

1	cup all-purpose flour
1½	teaspoons salt
½	teaspoon pepper
2	pounds sirloin steak, cut into strips
½	cup butter, melted
2	tablespoons butter
1	(8-ounce) package sliced fresh mushrooms
1	small onion, chopped
2	garlic cloves, minced
½	cup dry sherry or dry white wine
3	cups beef broth
2	tablespoons tomato paste
1	tablespoon Dijon mustard
1	tablespoon Worcestershire sauce
1	(16-ounce) container sour cream

Hot cooked egg noodles or mashed potatoes
Chopped fresh parsley

Combine first 3 ingredients in a large zip-top plastic freezer bag; add steak. Seal bag, and shake until meat is coated.

Brown meat in ½ cup butter in a sauté pan or large skillet over medium-high heat. Remove meat from pan; cover and keep warm. Add 2 tablespoons butter to hot pan; sauté mushrooms, onion, and garlic until browned and tender. Remove from pan; keep warm.

Add sherry or wine to pan; cook over high heat, stirring to loosen particles from bottom of pan. Add beef broth and next 3 ingredients, stirring until smooth. Return meat and sautéed mushroom mixture to pan; cook over medium heat until thickened, stirring frequently. Stir in sour cream; cook just until thoroughly heated. Serve over egg noodles or mashed potatoes; sprinkle with parsley. **Yield: 6 to 8 servings.**

Lemon-Garlic Roast Chicken
With Sautéed Green Beans

prep: 10 min.   bake: 1 hr., 10 min.   stand: 10 min.   cook: 7 min.

After roasting the chicken, sauté some green beans in the rich pan juices.

3   tablespoons chopped fresh parsley
2   tablespoons butter, softened
2   tablespoons olive oil
2   teaspoons lemon zest
2   garlic cloves, pressed
1   teaspoon salt
½   teaspoon pepper
1   (4-pound) whole chicken
1   (12-ounce) bag fresh green beans
    or 1 (16-ounce) package frozen whole
    green beans
Salt and pepper to taste
Garnishes: lemon wedges, fresh parsley sprigs

Preheat oven to 450°. Stir together first 7 ingredients. Starting at neck cavity, loosen skin from chicken breast and drumsticks by inserting fingers and gently pushing between skin and meat. (Do not completely detach skin.) Rub half of butter mixture under skin.

Tie ends of legs together with string; tuck wing tips under. Spread remaining half of butter mixture over chicken. Place chicken, breast side up, on a lightly greased rack in a lightly greased shallow roasting pan.

Bake at 450° for 30 minutes.

Reduce oven temperature to 350°, and bake 40 minutes or until a meat thermometer inserted into thigh registers 170°. Cover chicken loosely with aluminum foil to prevent excessive browning, if necessary. Remove chicken to a serving platter, reserving drippings in pan. Cover chicken with foil, and let stand 10 minutes before slicing.

Bring pan juices to a boil in a large skillet; add green beans, and cook 5 to 7 minutes or to desired tenderness. Season with salt and pepper to taste. Serve beans on platter with chicken. Garnish, if desired. **Yield: 4 servings.**

The Perfect Burgers

prep: 10 min.   stand: 35 min.   grill: 16 min.

A simple, rustic burger right off the grill is every man's favorite dish.

1½ pounds ground beef (75/25 or 25% fat)
1½ teaspoons kosher salt
1½ teaspoons coarsely ground pepper
6   (1-ounce) Cheddar cheese slices
6   hamburger buns
Toppings: lettuce leaves, red onion slices,
    tomato slices

Preheat grill to 350° to 400° (medium-high). Gently combine beef, salt, and pepper. Shape into 6 (4-inch) 1-inch-thick patties. Using thumb and forefinger, lightly press middle of patties, pressing in but not completely through, creating an indentation in center of patties. Let stand at room temperature 30 minutes.

Grill, covered with grill lid, over medium-high heat (350° to 400°) 6 to 7 minutes on each side or until no longer pink in center. Top each burger with 1 cheese slice, and grill, covered with grill lid, 1 to 2 minutes or until cheese is melted. Remove from grill, and let stand 5 minutes. Serve on hamburger buns with desired toppings. **Yield: 6 burgers.**

French Fries

prep: 30 min.   cook: 7 min. per batch

These russet strips are twice-fried for extra-crispy results.

4   pounds russet or Idaho potatoes, peeled
Vegetable oil
Salt to taste

Cut potatoes into ¼-inch-wide strips.
Pour vegetable oil to a depth of 4 inches in a Dutch oven, and heat to 325°. Fry potato strips, in batches, until lightly golden but not brown, 4 to 5 minutes per batch. Drain strips on paper towels.

Heat oil to 375°. Fry strips, in small batches, until golden brown and crisp, 1 to 2 minutes per batch. Drain on clean paper towels. Sprinkle strips with salt, and serve immediately. **Yield: 6 servings.**

variation

Salt-and-Pepper Fries: Prepare French Fries as directed. Grind some fresh pepper over hot fries after you sprinkle them with salt.

In summers past, when I was a little girl with pigtails, my dad and I used to play catch on the back deck while he would grill the world's best hamburgers. When he'd turn his back to flip the burgers, I would often sneak a sip of his cold beer. I'm sure he never knew…

—Julie Gunter, Food Editor

Basic Buttermilk Cornbread

prep: 10 min.   bake: 38 min.

¼   cup butter
1½ cups buttermilk
1   large egg
2   cups self-rising cornmeal

Preheat oven to 425°. Melt butter in a 10-inch cast-iron skillet in oven 8 minutes.

Whisk together buttermilk and egg in a large bowl; add melted butter from skillet, whisking until blended. Whisk in cornmeal until smooth. Spoon into hot skillet.

Bake at 425° for 30 minutes or until golden. Cut into wedges to serve.

Yield: 8 servings.

Fried Hot Dogs

prep: 5 min. cook: 4 min.

Try these skillet-fried dogs on hamburger buns with popular burger toppings, or use hot dog buns and chop the toppings instead of slicing. Or skip the toppings, and douse the dogs with the chili featured below.

4   hot dogs
¼   cup mayonnaise
¼   cup mustard
4   hamburger buns, toasted
4   tomato slices
4   onion slices
4   lettuce leaves

Cut a slit lengthwise in each hot dog, cutting to, but not through, other side. Place hot dogs, flat sides down, in a skillet, and cook over medium-high heat 2 minutes on each side or until well browned. Drain hot dogs on paper towels, if desired.

Stir together mayonnaise and mustard; spread on bun halves. Place 1 hot dog on bottom half of each bun. Top with tomato, onion, lettuce, and remaining bun halves. **Yield: 4 servings.**

Hot Dog Chili

prep: 10 min. cook: 1 hr.

Serve on hot dogs along with a pile of shredded Cheddar and finely chopped onion.

2   pounds lean ground beef
1   small onion, finely chopped
1   teaspoon vegetable oil
1   teaspoon salt
4   teaspoons chili powder
1   cup ketchup
4   teaspoons Worcestershire sauce
1   teaspoon white vinegar
½   teaspoon dry mustard
¼   to ½ teaspoon pepper

Cook ground beef in a Dutch oven over medium-high heat, stirring until beef crumbles and is no longer pink; drain well. Wipe Dutch oven clean with a paper towel.

Sauté onion in hot oil in Dutch oven 5 minutes. Add salt, chili powder, and beef, and cook 3 to 5 minutes. Stir in 2¼ cups water, ketchup, and next 4 ingredients. Bring to a boil; reduce heat to low, and simmer, stirring occasionally, 45 minutes or until most of liquid evaporates. **Yield: 5 cups.**

Egg Salad Sandwiches

prep: 13 min.

You can also use this egg salad to make finger sandwiches on thin white bread; or smear it on crostini, and top it with fresh herbs.

6	large hard-cooked eggs
2	tablespoons finely chopped celery
2	tablespoons sweet pickle relish
3	tablespoons mayonnaise
1	tablespoon grated onion
¾	teaspoon dried salad seasoning*
½	teaspoon Dijon mustard
¼	teaspoon salt
¼	teaspoon sugar
¼	teaspoon freshly ground pepper
½	cup sliced pimiento-stuffed green olives
6	bread slices

Mash 3 eggs in a large bowl using a fork or pastry blender. Chop remaining 3 eggs. Add chopped eggs, celery, and next 8 ingredients to mashed eggs; stir until blended. Gently stir in olives. Cover and chill, if desired. Divide egg salad among 3 bread slices; top with remaining bread slices. **Yield: 3 sandwiches.**

*For testing purposes only, we used McCormick Salad Supreme Seasoning.

Chicken Pot Pie

prep: 20 min.   cook: 14 min.   bake: 40 min.

A rich, flaky browned crust beckons you to dive into this comfort meal. Serving individual pot pies makes dinner an occasion.

½	cup butter
½	cup all-purpose flour
1½	cups chicken broth
1½	cups half-and-half
¾	teaspoon salt
½	teaspoon freshly ground pepper
2	tablespoons butter
1	(8-ounce) package sliced fresh mushrooms

Salt and pepper to taste

1	small onion, chopped
1	cup frozen green peas
3½	cups chopped cooked chicken
2	hard-cooked eggs, chopped
1	(15-ounce) package refrigerated piecrusts
1	tablespoon whipping cream
1	large egg, lightly beaten

Melt ½ cup butter in a heavy saucepan over low heat; whisk in flour, whisking until smooth. Cook, whisking constantly, 1 minute. Gradually add chicken broth and half-and-half; cook over medium heat, stirring constantly, until thickened and bubbly. Stir in ¾ teaspoon salt and ½ teaspoon pepper; set white sauce aside.

Melt 1 tablespoon butter in a large skillet over medium-high heat; add mushrooms, season lightly with salt and pepper, and sauté 10 minutes or until nicely browned. Don't overstir. Add mushrooms to white sauce. Add remaining 1 tablespoon butter to skillet. Add onion; sauté until tender. Stir in peas. Add vegetable mixture, chicken, and chopped eggs to white sauce.

Preheat oven to 375°. Fit 1 piecrust into a 9-inch deep-dish pieplate according to package directions. Spoon filling into crust; top with remaining piecrust. Trim off excess pastry. Fold edges under, and flute. Cut slits in top. Combine cream and egg; brush egg wash over pastry.

Bake at 375° for 30 to 40 minutes or until browned and bubbly. **Yield: 6 servings.**

Note: To make individual pot pies, spoon filling into 6 lightly greased 1-cup baking dishes. Cut out 6 circles of piecrust dough slightly larger than diameter of baking dishes. Top each dish with a round of dough; fold edges under, and flute. Cut slits in tops. Brush with egg wash. Bake at 375° for 30 to 35 minutes or until browned and bubbly.

Parmesan Chicken Salad

prep: 10 min.   cook: 16 min.

When you blend Parmesan, garlic, toasted pecans, and spicy brown mustard with chopped chicken, you get one fabulous chicken salad. It's even better the second day.

4	skinned and boned chicken breasts
1	teaspoon salt
½	teaspoon pepper
2	tablespoons vegetable oil
¾	cup freshly grated Parmesan cheese
½	cup chopped pecans, toasted
½	cup chopped celery
⅓	cup chopped green onions
¾	cup mayonnaise
2	tablespoons spicy brown mustard
1	garlic clove, pressed

Garnish: curly leaf lettuce

Sprinkle chicken with salt and pepper. Cook chicken in hot oil in a large skillet over medium-high heat 7 to 8 minutes on each side or until done; cool. Chop chicken.

Stir together chopped chicken, cheese, and next 3 ingredients.

Stir together mayonnaise, mustard, and garlic. Add to chicken salad; stir well. Cover and chill, if desired. Garnish serving plate, if desired.

Yield: 4½ cups.

Grilled Beer-Cheese Sandwich

prep: 5 min. cook: 10 min.

The common grilled cheese sandwich gets fancy with amber beer in the filling.

2   teaspoons butter, softened
2   bread slices
¼   cup Beer-Cheese Spread

Spread 1 teaspoon softened butter on 1 side of 2 bread slices. Place bread slices, buttered sides down, on wax paper. Spread Beer-Cheese Spread onto unbuttered side of 1 bread slice. Top with remaining bread slice, buttered side up. Cook sandwich in a nonstick skillet or on a griddle over medium heat 3 to 5 minutes on each side or until golden brown and cheese is melted. **Yield: 1 sandwich.**

Beer-Cheese Spread

prep: 15 min. chill: 2 hr.

This easy recipe (a tasty cousin of pimiento cheese) makes a lot, but the spread can be frozen up to a month; thaw it overnight in the refrigerator. It fits perfectly into four 10-ounce ramekins for gift giving. Try the spread over French fries, hot dogs, and chili, too.

1   (2-pound) block sharp Cheddar cheese,
     shredded
1   small onion, minced
2   garlic cloves, minced
½   teaspoon hot sauce
¼   teaspoon ground red pepper
1   (12-ounce) bottle amber beer, at room
     temperature*
Salt and pepper to taste
Garnish: fresh thyme sprig

Beat first 5 ingredients at low speed with a heavy-duty electric stand mixer until blended. Gradually add beer, beating until blended after each addition. Beat at medium-high speed 1 minute or until blended and creamy. Season with salt and pepper to taste. Cover and chill 2 hours. Garnish, if desired. Store in an airtight container in refrigerator up to 2 weeks. **Yield: 5 cups.**

*For testing purposes only, we used Abita Amber Beer.

Slow-Cooker BBQ Pork

prep: 5 min.   cook: 7 hr.

This super-simple recipe delivers big flavor. Reduce the fat but not the flavor in this juicy cut of pork by preparing it a day ahead. Cool the barbecue, and refrigerate overnight. Remove and discard any solidified fat before reheating.

1   (3- to 4-pound) shoulder pork roast
1   (18-ounce) bottle barbecue sauce*
1   (12-ounce) can cola soft drink

Place pork roast in a 6-quart slow cooker; pour barbecue sauce and cola over roast.
Cover with lid, and cook on HIGH 6 to 7 hours or until meat is tender and shreds easily. Serve on buns with slaw or over hot toasted cornbread.
Yield: 6 servings.

*For testing purposes only, we used Sticky Fingers Memphis Original Barbecue Sauce.

Note: If you don't have a slow cooker, place roast in a lightly greased Dutch oven; stir together barbecue sauce and cola, and pour over roast. Before placing lid on top of Dutch oven, cover roast with a double layer of aluminum foil. Bake, tightly covered, at 325° for 3½ hours or until tender.

Memphis-Style Coleslaw

prep: 7 min.   chill: 2 hr.

2   cups mayonnaise
¼   cup sugar
¼   cup Dijon mustard
¼   cup cider vinegar
1½ to 2 tablespoons celery seeds
1   teaspoon salt
⅛   teaspoon pepper
1   medium cabbage, shredded, or
    3 (10-ounce) bags finely shredded cabbage
2   large carrots, grated
1   green bell pepper, diced
2   tablespoons grated onion

Stir together first 7 ingredients in a large bowl; add cabbage and remaining ingredients, tossing gently. Cover and chill 2 to 3 hours; serve with a slotted spoon. **Yield: 12 servings.**

Ribs & Relations

I love the Fourth of July. For me it's so much more than paid time off with fireworks. It is *the* summer day for families and feasts. It involves the truly serious business of ribs and relations, food and traditions—the best-laid fires, hickory-smoked ribs, card games, potato salad, coleslaw, baked beans, corn on the cob, homemade ice cream, and lots of laughter.

For years our celebration headquarters was Aunt Wilda and Uncle Jack's house. Their backyard met all the requirements. It was large, flat, and shady, with a huge brick barbecue pit. There were open spaces for rolling and tumbling in the grass and areas under trees for blankets.

A large family we were not (10 adults and 4 children), but what we lacked in number, we habitually made up for in enthusiasm. Get us all together, and you had a group that could take its show on the road. Then, as now, we routinely cooked as if for an army. All the recipes, especially those for ribs and side dishes, invariably ended with the phrase "just in case."

Festivities at Wilda and Jack's always started early. Members of the other four households arrived with enough provisions to last for days: a box of ribs and chicken already cleaned, trimmed, and carefully submerged in a vinegary marinade. While skilled hands created fantastic dishes, I was the designated taster.

Aunt Wilda produced an entire vat of slow-cooked barbecue sauce. The tomato-based concoction—spicy, lemony, and hot—was so wonderful I could drink it by the cupful. It left a warm afterglow, like the long finish of a good Cabernet. There was no specific recipe. "I just shake and taste until it's right," she'd say. And it was the perfect blend of flavors year after savory year.

My dad, Uncle Jack, and Uncle C shared pit watch, turning the meat, mopping it with sauce, adding hickory, dousing flare-ups, and swapping jokes. The pit crew shifted slabs of ribs to make room for our midday hot dogs. No wiener ever tasted as good as those: plump, partly charred, and tucked into a smoky bun with a generous mop of Wilda's barbecue sauce. But the real reward—sheer dining ecstasy—came when the pit crew deemed the ribs ready. Tender and juicy with slightly crisp edges, they were the centerpiece of all the fabulous Hawkins-Scott family Fourths.

At day's end, ribs and fixings aplenty were packed to go home to each house. While the other kids waited for fireworks, I supervised the bottling of the sauce so Aunt Wilda would give me a jar of my own. For weeks after, I rationed out the potion to flavor my hamburgers and hot dogs.

Today's cast of characters has moved from a backyard into my dining room, and other things have changed as well. I demand that everyone arrive empty-handed so that I can show off my culinary skills. The tables are set with linens, china, and flowers; jazz piano, courtesy of compact discs, has long replaced raucous rock music. Imported beers now share space with the Buffalo Rock in the ice chest. Not quite everything is different, though. Only 16 people may be expected, but I still prepare enough food for 50. "Just in case."

Three of the original pit crew are no longer with us, but to this day we talk as if they were. Tales of them warm our hearts and keep us laughing, and those moments—so much more than a mere menu—are what fuel these rich family gatherings. The most important thing we celebrate is the ability to be together on one perfect summer day.

—Andria Scott Hurst, Former Senior Writer

Classic Barbecue Ribs

prep: 15 min.   cook: 7 hr.

It's comforting to know that ribs this good can come from a slow cooker. Put the ribs on to cook before you leave for work; or cook them overnight, and then refrigerate them until dinnertime.

4	pounds bone-in country-style pork ribs
2	teaspoons salt, divided
1	medium onion, chopped
1	cup firmly packed light brown sugar
1	cup apple butter
1	cup ketchup
½	cup lemon juice
½	cup orange juice
1	tablespoon steak sauce*
1	teaspoon coarsely ground pepper
1	teaspoon minced garlic
½	teaspoon Worcestershire sauce

Cut ribs apart, if necessary, and trim excess fat; sprinkle 1 teaspoon salt over ribs.
Stir together remaining 1 teaspoon salt, onion, and next 9 ingredients until blended. Pour half of onion mixture into a 5-quart slow cooker. Place ribs in slow cooker, and pour remaining mixture over ribs.
Cover with lid, and cook on HIGH 6 to 7 hours or until ribs are tender. **Yield: 4 to 6 servings.**

*For testing purposes only, we used A.1.

Note: If you make this recipe a day ahead, refrigerate ribs overnight and remove fat from sauce before reheating. If you reheat ribs in the microwave, use 50% power.

Greek Pizza

Greek Pizza

prep: 15 min.   bake: 14 min.

Greek salad ingredients merge with hummus on this innovative pizza that's packed with flavor.

1   (12-inch) prebaked pizza crust
1   cup deli hummus
1   pint grape tomatoes
1   cup pitted kalamata olives
½   cup pepperoncini rings, drained
½   cup chopped red onion
¾   cup coarsely crumbled feta cheese
2   tablespoons olive oil (optional)
1   tablespoon fresh oregano leaves
      (optional)

Preheat oven to 450°. Spread crust with hummus. Arrange grape tomatoes and next 3 ingredients over pizza. Sprinkle with feta cheese.
Bake directly on oven rack at 450° for 12 to 14 minutes or until feta cheese is lightly browned. Drizzle with olive oil, and sprinkle with oregano before serving, if desired. **Yield: 4 servings.**

Note: For added depth of flavor, drizzle the tomatoes and chopped red onion with 1 tablespoon olive oil, and roast on a baking sheet at 475° for 8 to 10 minutes before adding to pizza.

Ultimate Cheese Pizza

prep: 10 min.   bake: 14 min.

Shred any leftover cheese you find in the fridge for this simple pie.

1   (14.5-ounce) can whole tomatoes, drained
      and chopped
1   teaspoon bottled minced garlic
1   (12-inch) prebaked pizza crust
2   cups (8 ounces) mixed shredded cheese

Preheat oven to 450°. Stir together tomatoes and garlic. Spread crust with tomato mixture, and sprinkle with cheese.
Bake directly on oven rack at 450° for 12 to 14 minutes or until cheese is melted. **Yield: 4 servings.**

variations

Ultimate Cheeseburger Pizza: Substitute 1½ cups shredded Cheddar cheese for 2 cups mixed shredded cheese. Prepare Ultimate Cheese Pizza, sprinkling 1½ cups cooked and crumbled ground beef (about ½ pound), ¼ cup chopped green onions, and ½ teaspoon salt over tomato mixture. Sprinkle with cheese. Bake as directed. Serve with pickles, if desired.

Ultimate Veggie Pizza: Prepare Ultimate Cheese Pizza, arranging 2 cups roasted or grilled vegetables over tomato mixture. Sprinkle with cheese. Bake as directed.

Chili-Style Spaghetti and Meatballs

prep: 20 min.   bake: 15 min.   cook: 20 min.

Discover a new flavor direction for an old classic. If desired, freeze leftovers in single servings: spaghetti, three meatballs, and sauce.

1½ pounds ground round
1   tablespoon grated onion
1   teaspoon salt
1   teaspoon ground cumin
12 ounces uncooked spaghetti
1   tablespoon chili powder
2   teaspoons olive oil
1   (14½-ounce) can diced tomatoes, undrained
1   (14-ounce) can beef broth
1   (6-ounce) can tomato paste
1   (4.5-ounce) can chopped green chiles
1   (15-ounce) can black beans, rinsed and drained
Toppings: sour cream, shredded Cheddar cheese, chopped red onion

Preheat oven to 350°. Combine ground round and next 3 ingredients in a large bowl just until blended. Gently shape meat mixture into 18 (1½-inch) balls.

Place a lightly greased rack in an aluminum foil-lined broiler pan, and arrange meatballs on rack.

Bake at 350° for 15 minutes or until browned. (Centers will be slightly pink.)

Prepare spaghetti according to package directions. Keep warm.

Cook chili powder in hot oil in a Dutch oven over medium heat, stirring constantly, 2 minutes. Stir in tomatoes and next 3 ingredients. Gently stir meatballs into tomato mixture. Bring to a boil; cover, reduce heat, and simmer, stirring occasionally, 10 minutes. Gently stir in beans, and cook 3 more minutes. Serve immediately with spaghetti and desired toppings.

Yield: 6 servings.

Cola Pot Roast

prep: 30 min.   chill: 8 hr.   cook: 12 min.   bake: 4 hr.

Instead of broth, cola is used for cooking this roast. It adds a slightly sweet flavor note to the meat and vegetables. Grind some fresh pepper over the roast before serving, if desired.

1   (12-ounce) can cola soft drink
1   medium onion, chopped
8   garlic cloves, minced
1   lemon, thinly sliced
1   cup soy sauce
3   tablespoons vegetable oil, divided
1   (3- to 4-pound) boneless chuck roast, trimmed
1   teaspoon fresh coarsely ground pepper
8   large carrots (about 1½ pounds), cut into 1½-inch chunks
7   Yukon gold potatoes (about 2¼ pounds), cut into quarters
2   large onions, cut into eighths
2   tablespoons cornstarch
Garnish: fresh oregano or thyme sprigs

Combine first 5 ingredients and 2 tablespoons oil in a large zip-top plastic freezer bag. Add roast, turning to coat. Seal and chill 8 to 24 hours. Remove roast from marinade; discard lemon slices, and reserve marinade. Sprinkle roast with pepper.

Brown roast 4 minutes on each side in remaining 1 tablespoon hot oil in a large skillet over medium-high heat. Remove roast from skillet, and transfer to a large roasting pan. Add reserved marinade to skillet, stirring to loosen particles from bottom. Bring to a boil. Remove from heat.

Preheat oven to 300°. Arrange carrots, potatoes, and onions around roast in pan; pour hot marinade over roast and vegetables. Cover and bake at 300° for 4 hours or until meat and vegetables are tender. Transfer roast and vegetables to a serving platter. Skim fat from juices in roasting pan.

Whisk together cornstarch and ½ cup cold water in a small bowl until smooth. Whisk cornstarch mixture into juices in pan; cook over medium-high heat 3 minutes or until thickened, whisking to loosen particles. Serve gravy with roast and vegetables. Garnish, if desired. **Yield: 6 to 8 servings.**

Chicken-Fried Steak

prep: 10 min.   cook: 42 min.

Authentic chicken-fried steak is crunchy outside, tender inside, and served with plenty of cream gravy made from pan drippings. Bring it on!

¼ teaspoon salt

¼ teaspoon ground black pepper

6 (4-ounce) cube steaks

38 saltine crackers (1 sleeve), crushed

1¼ cups all-purpose flour, divided

½ teaspoon baking powder

2 teaspoons salt, divided

1½ teaspoons ground black pepper, divided

½ teaspoon ground red pepper

4¾ cups milk, divided

2 large eggs

3½ cups peanut oil

Sprinkle ¼ teaspoon each salt and black pepper over steaks. Set aside.

Combine cracker crumbs, 1 cup flour, baking powder, 1 teaspoon salt, ½ teaspoon black pepper, and red pepper.

Whisk together ¾ cup milk and eggs. Dredge steaks in cracker crumb mixture; dip in milk mixture, and dredge in cracker mixture again.

Preheat oven to 225°. Pour oil into a 12-inch skillet; heat to 360°. (Do not use a nonstick skillet.) Fry steaks, in batches, 10 minutes. Turn and fry each batch 4 to 5 more minutes or until golden brown. Remove to a wire rack on a jelly-roll pan. Keep steaks warm in a 225° oven. Carefully drain hot oil, reserving cooked bits and 1 tablespoon drippings in skillet.

Whisk together remaining ¼ cup flour, 1 teaspoon salt, 1 teaspoon black pepper, and 4 cups milk. Pour mixture into reserved drippings in skillet; cook over medium-high heat, whisking constantly, 10 to 12 minutes or until thickened. Serve gravy with steaks and mashed potatoes.
Yield: 6 servings.

At my parents' house, no vegetable except mashed potatoes goes on the chicken-fried plate unless Mom requires it.

—Vanessa McNeil Rocchio, Test Kitchens Specialist

Pan-Fried Pork Chops

prep: 10 min. cook: 2 min. per batch

½   cup all-purpose flour
1   teaspoon salt
1   teaspoon seasoned pepper
1½ pounds wafer-thin boneless pork chops
¼   cup vegetable oil

Combine first 3 ingredients in a shallow dish; dredge pork chops in flour mixture.

Fry pork chops, in 3 batches, in hot oil in a large skillet over medium-high heat 1 minute on each side or until browned. Drain on paper towels. **Yield: 6 to 8 servings.**

Chicken and Dumplings

prep: 15 min.   cook: 25 min.

Deli-roasted chicken and canned biscuits make a tasty speed-scratch version of this familiar old favorite. One roasted chicken yields about three cups of meat.

1   (32-ounce) container low-sodium chicken broth
1   (14½-ounce) can low-sodium chicken broth
3   cups shredded cooked chicken (about 1½ pounds)
1   (10¾-ounce) can reduced-fat cream of celery soup
¼   teaspoon poultry seasoning
2   hard-cooked eggs, chopped
1   (10.2-ounce) can refrigerated jumbo buttermilk biscuits
Garnish: chopped fresh parsley

Stir together first 5 ingredients in a Dutch oven over medium-high heat; bring to a boil. Reduce heat to low; simmer, stirring occasionally, 15 minutes. Add chopped eggs.

Place biscuits on a lightly floured surface. Roll or pat each biscuit to ⅛-inch thickness; cut into ½-inch-wide strips.

Return broth mixture to a low boil over medium-high heat. Drop strips, 1 at a time, into boiling broth. Reduce heat to low; simmer 10 minutes, stirring occasionally to prevent dumplings from sticking. Garnish, if desired. **Yield: 4 to 6 servings.**

Pork Chops, Cabbage, and Apples

prep: 20 min.   cook: 49 min.

Pork, cabbage, and apples make a classic combination that's really delightful.

3   teaspoons paprika, divided
2   teaspoons chopped fresh or 1 teaspoon dried thyme, divided
2   teaspoons kosher salt, divided
1½ teaspoons freshly ground pepper, divided
2   teaspoons chopped fresh or 1 teaspoon dried sage, divided
6   (½-inch-thick) bone-in pork loin chops
2   bacon slices
1   head cabbage (about 2 pounds), coarsely chopped
2   medium onions, thinly sliced
1   large Granny Smith apple, peeled and sliced
1   tablespoon tomato paste
1   (12-ounce) bottle lager beer*
Garnish: fresh thyme sprigs

Combine 2 teaspoons paprika, 1 teaspoon fresh or ½ teaspoon dried thyme, 1 teaspoon salt, 1 teaspoon pepper, and 1 teaspoon fresh or ½ teaspoon dried sage; rub over pork chops.
Cook bacon slices in a large, deep skillet over medium-high heat 6 to 8 minutes or until crisp; remove bacon, and drain on paper towels, reserving drippings in skillet. Crumble bacon.
Cook pork in hot drippings 3 minutes on each side or until browned and done; remove pork from skillet, and keep warm.
Add cabbage, onions, and apple to skillet. Cover and reduce heat to medium; cook, stirring occasionally, 15 minutes or until cabbage begins to wilt. Add tomato paste, beer, bacon, remaining 1 teaspoon paprika, 1 teaspoon fresh or ½ teaspoon dried thyme, 1 teaspoon salt, ½ teaspoon pepper, and 1 teaspoon fresh or ½ teaspoon dried sage, stirring to loosen particles from bottom of skillet. Cover and cook 15 minutes or until cabbage is tender and liquid is slightly thickened. Add pork, and cook, uncovered, 5 minutes or until thoroughly heated. Garnish, if desired. **Yield: 6 servings.**

*For testing purposes only, we used Samuel Adams Boston Lager; 1½ cups apple cider may be substituted.

Fried Lemon-Rosemary Catfish

prep: 10 min.   chill: 1 hr.   cook: 8 min.

Fresh herb flavor and a squirt of citrus send fried catfish uptown. You can still add tartar sauce.

1	large lemon
¼	cup milk
2	medium eggs, beaten
2	tablespoons chopped fresh rosemary
2	tablespoons minced fresh garlic
4	(4- to 6-ounce) catfish fillets
2	cups yellow cornmeal
¼	cup olive oil

Garnishes: lemon wedges, fresh rosemary sprigs

Grate zest from lemon, avoiding the pale bitter pith, into a large bowl; squeeze lemon juice into bowl. Stir in milk and next 3 ingredients until blended.

Rinse fillets, and pat dry with paper towels. Add fillets to lemon mixture in bowl; cover and chill 1 hour.

Place cornmeal on a large plate or in a large shallow dish. Turn fillets in lemon mixture until thoroughly coated; dredge in cornmeal, coating evenly.

Cook fillets in hot oil in a large skillet over medium-high heat 4 minutes on each side or until browned. Remove from skillet. Garnish, if desired. **Yield: 4 servings.**

BLT Potato Salad

prep: 20 min.   cook: 20 min.   chill: 3 hr.

Potato salad—pure and simple—remains one of the tastiest icons of a Southern picnic. Merging it with the flavors of a BLT is a real treat.

3	large baking potatoes (about 3½ pounds), peeled and chopped
1	cup mayonnaise
3	tablespoons sweet pickle relish
2	tablespoons Dijon mustard
¼	cup chopped fresh flat-leaf parsley
1	teaspoon salt
1	teaspoon freshly ground pepper
4	green onions, sliced
2	hard-cooked eggs, coarsely chopped
1	cup grape tomatoes, halved
8	bacon slices, cooked and crumbled

Curly leaf lettuce leaves

Bring potatoes and salted water to cover to a boil in a Dutch oven. Boil 15 to 20 minutes or until tender (do not overcook). Drain and cool. **Stir** together mayonnaise and next 5 ingredients in a large bowl; add cooked potatoes, green onions, and eggs, tossing gently until well blended. Gently stir in tomatoes. Cover and chill at least 3 hours. Stir in bacon just before serving. Serve on lettuce leaves. **Yield: 8 to 10 servings.**

My pimiento cheese recipe was originally that of my great-grandmother Kersh, who lived until she was 98 years old—slim, trim, and fearless of fat content. One tip worth passing along: Use a box grater to achieve both coarse-grated and finely shredded cheese.

—Mary Allen Perry, Associate Food Editor

Pimiento Cheese Panini

prep: 15 min. cook: 4 min. per batch

It's tough to deny the simple pleasure of this classic cheese spread, especially when it's slathered onto crusty peasant bread and then grilled.

¾ cup mayonnaise*

1 (4-ounce) jar diced pimiento, drained

1 teaspoon Worcestershire sauce

1 teaspoon finely grated onion

¼ teaspoon ground red pepper

1 (8-ounce) block extra-sharp Cheddar cheese, finely shredded

1 (8-ounce) block sharp Cheddar cheese, shredded

2 medium jalapeño peppers, seeded and minced (optional)

2 (16-ounce) loaves ciabatta bread

Olive oil

Stir together first 5 ingredients in a large bowl; stir in cheeses and, if desired, jalapeño. Store in refrigerator up to 1 week.

Slice bread into 20 (½-inch-thick) diagonal slices. Spread half of slices with pimiento cheese. Top with remaining slices. Brush outside of bread slices with olive oil.

Preheat panini press. Grill sandwiches, in batches, 3 to 4 minutes or until golden brown and cheese is melted. Cut sandwiches in half, if desired. **Yield: 10 sandwiches.**

*For testing purposes only, we used Duke's Mayonnaise.

Raised on Fried Chicken

Fried chicken feeds the soul of the South. This regional favorite ranks right up there with God, Mama, and country. Authors have penned tomes on the subject. Feuds have erupted over whose fried chicken tastes the best. Some cooks even guard their recipes with the zeal of armed guards at Fort Knox.

Now, some might consider it folly to step into the midst of such a debate. Not me. I was raised on fried chicken. I learned the recipe at my mother's elbow. On occasion, I was even called upon to select dinner from my very own feathered flock. So I know chicken. It's as much a part of me as my eye color.

—Cassandra Vanhooser, Associate Livings Editor

{ portable }
Mama's Fried Chicken

**prep: 30 min.   chill: 2 hr.
cook: 30 min. per batch**

1   (3- to 4-pound) whole chicken, cut into pieces
1   teaspoon salt
1   teaspoon pepper
2   cups buttermilk
Self-rising flour
Vegetable oil
Salt (optional)

Sprinkle chicken with 1 teaspoon each salt and pepper. Place chicken in a shallow dish or zip-top plastic freezer bag, and add buttermilk. Cover or seal, and chill at least 2 hours.
Remove chicken from buttermilk, discarding buttermilk. Dredge chicken in flour.
Pour oil to a depth of 1½ inches in a deep skillet or Dutch oven; heat to 360°. Add chicken, a few pieces at a time; cover and cook 6 minutes. Uncover chicken, and cook 9 minutes. Turn chicken; cover and cook 6 minutes. Uncover and cook 5 to 9 minutes, turning chicken the last 3 minutes for even browning, if necessary. Drain on paper towels. Sprinkle lightly with salt while chicken is hot, if desired. **Yield: 4 to 6 servings.**

I've always thought that if I make it to heaven,
every meal will be fried chicken, fresh asparagus,
and strawberries.

—Florence Bishop, *Southern Living* Reader

breakfast anytime

Mama Faye's Biscuits

I'm lucky to have a husband who is easy to please. Even when we were newlyweds, Wayne always cleaned his plate and always bragged that my cooking was the best. That is, until three weeks into wedded bliss, when I attempted to bake my first from-scratch Southern biscuits.

I heaped the crumbly batch onto a platter and proudly set my offering on the table. When I glanced at Wayne, expecting more "attaboys," I saw instead a wistful look in his eyes. "Have I ever told you about Mama Faye's biscuits?" he whispered, lost in reveries of an East Texas kitchen and a grandmother who could do no wrong.

Of course I had heard about the biscuits. Whenever the Cook family gathers, talk *always* turns to Mama Faye's biscuits. Her biscuits have assumed mythic proportions, partly because of their 6-inch span and partly because their exact character—crackly on the outside, cakelike in the middle—has made a mockery of all imitators through the years. Still, as I studied Wayne's faraway gaze, I decided that, whatever it took, no matter how many Cooks before me had tried and failed, I would be the one to unlock the biscuit mystery.

My chance came at the next family reunion in Ore City, Texas. Standing in the kitchen among the gathered clan, I asked Mama Faye with all the casualness I could muster, "Can I take a look at your biscuit recipe?"

"Recipe? Mama Faye?" giggled Wayne's Aunt Nancy, tickled at the very sound of the words. "What's so funny about that?" I mumbled to myself, sensing I was on shaky ground. Reassessing my strategy, I pleaded, "Just tell me what's in it then." Mama Faye dusted off her flour-caked hands and looked at me earnestly: "Oh, I'm sure I can do that ... now let me see ... I put in flour, soda, salt, buttermilk—always buttermilk."

continued

"Now we're getting somewhere!" I exclaimed, grabbing my notebook. "Let's start at the beginning. How much flour?" I asked, poised to record every word.

"Oh, I don't rightly know," she slowly replied. "I just work it all in till it feels right."

Trouble was, I didn't know anything, except that my pilgrimage had ended at this Tower of Babel, with the two of us speaking gibberish. I wanted just the facts—calculations I could write down and memorize. She was speaking of feelings and intuition. "Really," the gentle wizard apologized, "I wish I could tell you, but I can't. I've been making biscuits for so long, I don't know *how* I do it. I just do it."

"That's it!" I jumped, recognizing the connection. "I'll just watch whatever you do."

"Yes, you're welcome to. I don't even use a spoon," she began, patting the mound of dough like a familiar friend. "Just my own two hands—that's all I need, and that's all you'll need, too."

Studying her movements with the intensity of a surgical intern, I tried to quantify her measurements. How much soda did she put in? What's a pinch or a scoop or a dab? She blended the ingredients like oils on a palette: a touch more soda, a tad more salt—just right. "Now it's your turn to try," she said, guiding my hands as we swirled buttermilk into the flour. "Work it easy now, not so rough," she urged.

Next, we gingerly placed each mound on a sheet spread thick with bacon grease and hot for the oven. Satisfied, she turned to me and said, "Now you try it yourself at home. You'll do just fine."

With Mama Faye's blessings and my detailed directions scrawled on floury, grease-spattered pages, Wayne and I set out for home. I kept those cryptic notes for years, but I've never attempted to decipher them. I understand now, after a decade or more, what Mama Faye had tried to tell me in her Texas kitchen. Cooking's not a science captured in formulas and rules, but a creative and personal art that's fueled by innovation and imagination—and even memory.

—Lynnmarie P. Cook, Former Assistant Food Editor

Nutty Granola

prep: 4 min.   bake: 25 min.

Enjoy this healthy snack sprinkled over yogurt for breakfast.

3   cups uncooked regular oats
½   cup flaked coconut or organic coconut chips
½   cup whole natural almonds
¼   cup regular or honey-crunch wheat germ
¼   cup sunflower kernels
¼   cup plus 2 tablespoons honey
¼   cup vegetable oil
2   tablespoons brown sugar
1   teaspoon vanilla extract
¼   teaspoon salt
¾   cup raisins

Preheat oven to 350°. Combine first 5 ingredients in a large bowl; stir well, and set aside.
Combine honey and next 4 ingredients; pour over oat mixture, and stir well. Spread granola mixture onto a lightly greased 15- x 10-inch jelly-roll pan.
Bake at 350° for 25 minutes or until golden, stirring every 5 minutes. Cool. Stir in raisins. Store in an airtight container in a cool, dry place up to 1½ months. **Yield: 5½ cups.**

Farmers Market Scramble

Farmers Market Scramble

prep: 10 min.   cook: 14 min.

Fresh herbs and tomato give these eggs a punch of flavor.

12	large eggs
¼	cup milk
¼	cup whipping cream
¾	teaspoon salt
¼	teaspoon freshly ground pepper
¼	teaspoon hot sauce
2	tablespoons butter
1	tomato, chopped and drained on a paper towel
¼	cup chopped fresh chives
2	tablespoons chopped fresh flat-leaf parsley

Whisk together first 6 ingredients in a large bowl until blended.

Melt 2 tablespoons butter in a large nonstick skillet over medium heat. Add egg mixture; cook, without stirring, until eggs begin to set on bottom. Draw a spatula across bottom of skillet to form large curds. Cook until eggs are thickened but still moist. (Do not stir constantly.) Remove from heat, and transfer to a warm platter. Sprinkle platter of eggs with tomato, chives, and parsley; serve hot. **Yield: 6 servings.**

Smoky Brown Sugar Bacon

prep: 12 min.   bake: 20 min. per batch

This bacon takes a little while to prepare, but it's more than worth it. Any bacon left after breakfast makes for primo sandwiches.

3	cups firmly packed light brown sugar
24	slices applewood smoked bacon

Preheat oven to 425°. Spread brown sugar onto a large plate; dredge half of bacon in sugar, pressing to be sure plenty of sugar sticks to both sides of bacon. Place bacon in a single layer on a large wire rack on an aluminum foil-lined rimmed baking sheet.

Bake at 425° for 18 to 20 minutes or until crisp. Remove bacon from rack to a serving platter or parchment paper to cool. Repeat with remaining bacon and brown sugar. **Yield: 24 slices.**

Note: We used 1½ (1-pound) packages Nueske's Applewood Smoked Bacon to yield the 24 slices; otherwise, any thick-cut bacon, smoked or not, would also work well in this recipe.

Pimiento Cheese Biscuits

prep: 20 min.   chill: 10 min.   bake: 15 min.

Any Southerner would be proud to have a bowl of these piping hot cheese biscuits on the breakfast table.

1   cup (4 ounces) shredded sharp Cheddar
     cheese
2¼ cups self-rising soft-wheat flour*
½   cup cold butter, cut into ¼-inch-thick slices
1   cup buttermilk
1   (4-ounce) jar diced pimiento, drained
Self-rising soft-wheat flour*
2   tablespoons melted butter

Combine shredded cheese and 2¼ cups flour in a large bowl.

Sprinkle butter slices over flour-cheese mixture; toss gently. Cut butter into flour with a pastry blender until crumbly and mixture resembles small peas. Cover and chill 10 minutes.

Combine buttermilk and diced pimiento; add buttermilk mixture to flour mixture, stirring just until dry ingredients are moistened.

Turn dough out onto a lightly floured surface, and knead 3 or 4 times, gradually adding additional flour as needed. With floured hands, press or pat dough into a ¾-inch-thick rectangle (about 9 x 5 inches). Sprinkle top of dough with additional flour. Fold dough over onto itself in 3 sections, starting with 1 short end. (Fold dough rectangle as if folding a letter-size piece of paper.) Repeat procedure 2 more times, beginning with pressing into a ¾-inch-thick dough rectangle (about 9 x 5 inches).

Preheat oven to 450°. Press or pat dough to ½-inch thickness on a lightly floured surface; cut with a 2-inch round cutter, and place, side by side, on a parchment paper-lined or lightly greased jelly-roll pan. (Dough rounds should touch.)

Bake at 450° for 13 to 15 minutes or until lightly browned. Remove from oven, and brush with 2 tablespoons melted butter. **Yield: 2½ dozen.**

*For testing purposes only, we used White Lily Self-Rising Soft-Wheat Flour.

Country Ham With Redeye Gravy

prep: 10 min.   cook: 29 min.

For true redeye gravy, Southerners use caffeinated coffee for its pick-me-up quality.

2   cups hot strong brewed coffee
¼   cup firmly packed brown sugar
2   (12-ounce) slices boneless country ham

Stir together coffee and sugar; let mixture cool.
Cook ham in a large cast-iron skillet over medium heat 5 to 7 minutes on each side or until browned. Remove ham, and keep warm, reserving drippings in skillet.
Add coffee mixture to skillet, stirring to loosen particles from bottom; bring to a boil. Boil, stirring occasionally, until reduced by half (about 15 minutes). Serve with ham. **Yield: 6 servings.**

Margaret's Creamy Grits

prep: 10 min.   cook: 10 min.

Former Test Kitchens Director Margaret Dickey had a knack for thick, rich grits.

2   cups half-and-half or whipping cream
¼   teaspoon salt
⅛   teaspoon granulated garlic
⅛   teaspoon pepper
½   cup uncooked quick-cooking grits
2   ounces cream cheese, cubed
¾   cup (3 ounces) shredded sharp Cheddar cheese
¼   teaspoon hot sauce

Bring first 4 ingredients to a boil in a Dutch oven; gradually stir in grits. Return to a boil; cover, reduce heat, and simmer, stirring occasionally, 5 to 7 minutes or until thickened. Add cheeses and hot sauce, stirring until cheeses melt. Serve hot. **Yield: 4 servings.**

Hash Brown Casserole

prep: 20 min.   bake: 1 hr.

This down-home side dish boasts a buttery cornflake crust on top.

¾   cup chopped onion
½   teaspoon paprika
½   teaspoon freshly ground pepper
1   (32-ounce) package frozen Southern-style
      hash brown potatoes (diced)
2   tablespoons butter, melted
1   (10¾-ounce) can condensed cream of
      chicken soup, undiluted
1   (8-ounce) package pasteurized prepared.
      cheese product, cubed
1   (8-ounce) carton sour cream
2½ cups cornflakes cereal, coarsely crushed
2   tablespoons butter, melted

Preheat oven to 350°. Combine first 5 ingredients in a large bowl; toss well.

Combine soup and cheese in a medium microwave-safe bowl. Microwave at HIGH 6 minutes or until cheese melts, stirring every 2 minutes. Stir in sour cream. Pour cheese mixture over potato mixture, and stir well. Spread into a lightly greased 13- x 9-inch baking dish.

Combine cornflakes and 2 tablespoons butter; sprinkle over top of potato mixture.

Bake, uncovered, at 350° for 1 hour. **Yield: 12 servings.**

Country Breakfast Casserole

prep: 10 min.   cook: 10 min.   bake: 45 min.   stand: 5 min.

1   pound ground mild pork sausage
1   teaspoon salt
1   cup uncooked quick-cooking grits
1½ cups (6 ounces) shredded Cheddar cheese,
      divided
4   large eggs, lightly beaten
¾   cup milk
¼   cup butter, melted
¼   teaspoon pepper

Preheat oven to 350°. Brown sausage in a large skillet over medium heat, stirring until it crumbles and is no longer pink; drain.

Bring 3½ cups water and salt to a boil in a medium saucepan; stir in grits. Return to a boil; cover, reduce heat, and simmer 5 minutes, stirring occasionally. Remove from heat; add 1 cup cheese, stirring until cheese melts. Stir in sausage, eggs, and next 3 ingredients.

Pour mixture into a greased 11- x 7-inch baking dish; sprinkle with remaining ½ cup cheese.

Bake, uncovered, at 350° for 45 minutes or until set. Let stand 5 minutes before serving. **Yield: 6 servings.**

Hash Brown Casserole

Cinnamon-Raisin Rolls

prep: 10 min.   stand: 45 min.   bake: 40 min.

These scrumptious breakfast rolls are made from a package of frozen biscuits. They're so easy to prepare, you don't even need a rolling pin.

1   (26.4-ounce) package frozen biscuits
All-purpose flour
¼   cup butter, softened
¾   cup firmly packed brown sugar
1   teaspoon ground cinnamon
1   cup golden raisins or raisins
½   cup chopped pecans, toasted
1   cup powdered sugar
3   tablespoons milk
½   teaspoon vanilla extract

Arrange frozen biscuits, with sides touching, in 3 rows of 4 biscuits on a lightly floured surface. Let stand 30 to 45 minutes or until biscuits are thawed but still cool to the touch.

Preheat oven to 375°. Sprinkle thawed biscuits lightly with flour. Press biscuit edges together, and pat to form a 10- x 12-inch rectangle of dough; spread with softened butter. Stir together brown sugar and cinnamon; sprinkle over butter. Sprinkle raisins and pecans over brown sugar mixture.

Roll up dough, starting at 1 long end; cut into 12 (about 1-inch-thick) slices. Place rolls in a lightly greased 10-inch cast-iron skillet, 10-inch round pan, or 9-inch square pan.

Bake at 375° for 35 to 40 minutes or until center rolls are golden brown and done; cool slightly.

Stir together powdered sugar, milk, and vanilla; drizzle over rolls. **Yield: 1 dozen.**

Note: For individual rolls, prepare as directed; place 1 slice in each of 12 lightly greased 3-inch muffin cups. Bake at 375° for 20 to 25 minutes or until golden brown. Cool slightly, and remove from pan. Drizzle with glaze.

Buttermilk 'n' Honey Pancakes

prep: 10 min.   cook: 3 min. per batch

Honey adds sweetness and moisture to these pancakes. Experiment by using dark or wildflower honey.

1   cup all-purpose flour
1   teaspoon baking powder
½   teaspoon baking soda
¼   teaspoon salt
1   large egg, lightly beaten
1   cup buttermilk
2   tablespoons honey
Pecan-Honey Butter (optional)

Stir together first 4 ingredients in a medium bowl. Add egg, buttermilk, and honey, stirring until well blended.

Pour ¼ cup batter onto a hot, lightly greased griddle or skillet. Cook 1 to 2 minutes or until top is covered with bubbles and edges look cooked. Turn and cook 1 more minute. Repeat with remaining batter. Top pancakes with Pecan-Honey Butter, if desired. Serve with syrup. **Yield: about 9 (3-inch) pancakes.**

Note: For 5 jumbo pancakes, use a heaping ⅓ cup batter for each pancake.

Pecan-Honey Butter

prep: 5 min.

Let the chilled Pecan-Honey Butter stand at room temperature 10 to 15 minutes to soften before serving.

½   cup butter, softened
⅓   cup finely chopped pecans, toasted
2   tablespoons honey
⅛   to ¼ teaspoon ground cinnamon

Stir together all ingredients until blended. Cover and chill until ready to serve. **Yield: about ¾ cup.**

When Don and I were married 44 years ago, we were given a unique wedding present: three blueberry bushes. Since that day, love has passed from our home to others through the blueberries we grow. We pick blueberries all summer and freeze them for this wonderful muffin recipe, which I make all year long to celebrate happy occasions and to help people who aren't feeling well.

—Laura Wallace, *Southern Living* Reader

Blueberry Sweet Muffins

prep: 10 min. bake: 25 min.

1½ cups all-purpose flour
½ cup sugar
2 teaspoons baking powder
½ teaspoon salt
⅓ cup milk
¼ cup vegetable oil
1 large egg
1 cup fresh or frozen blueberries
2 tablespoons sugar

Preheat oven to 400°. Combine first 4 ingredients in a large bowl; make a well in center of mixture. **Stir** together milk, oil, and egg; add to dry ingredients, stirring just until moistened. Fold in blueberries. Spoon into greased or paper-lined muffin pans, filling two-thirds full. Sprinkle batter with 2 tablespoons sugar. **Bake** at 400° for 20 to 25 minutes or until muffins are golden. Remove from pans immediately, and cool on wire racks. **Yield: 6 muffins.**

Poppy Seed-Lemon Muffins

prep: 10 min.   bake: 20 min.

These are good on-the-go muffins, since they don't have a glaze. Rest assured, they're still plenty sweet.

1	(18.25-ounce) package yellow cake mix with pudding*
⅔	cup vegetable oil
⅔	cup apricot nectar
4	large eggs
⅓	cup poppy seeds
½	teaspoon lemon zest
2½	tablespoons fresh lemon juice

Preheat oven to 400°. Combine all ingredients, stirring until blended. Spoon into greased or paper-lined muffin pans, filling two-thirds full. **Bake** at 400° for 18 to 20 minutes or until golden brown. Remove from pans immediately, and cool on wire racks. **Yield: about 2 dozen.**

*For testing purposes only, we used Betty Crocker Cake Mix.

Oatmeal Muffins

prep: 12 min.   bake: 15 min.

Instead of having oatmeal for breakfast, try these tender oat muffins dotted with dates.

¾	cup all-purpose flour
1	cup uncooked regular oats
½	cup chopped dates
¼	cup sugar
1	tablespoon baking powder
½	teaspoon salt
¾	cup milk
3	tablespoons butter, melted
1	large egg, lightly beaten
	Oats (optional)

Preheat oven to 425°. Combine first 6 ingredients in a large bowl; make a well in center of mixture. Stir together milk, butter, and egg; add to dry ingredients. Stir just until moistened.
Spoon batter into lightly greased or paper-lined muffin pans, filling two-thirds full. Sprinkle with oats, if desired.
Bake at 425° for 15 minutes. Remove from pans immediately. **Yield: 8 muffins.**

Note: We used 4-inch squares of parchment paper to fashion handmade paper muffin liners.

Growing up in my family, there was only one way to eat banana bread: doused with milk in a cereal bowl. Nowadays, it makes me smile to see _my_ children carry on the delectable, mushy tradition.

—Julie Gunter, Food Editor

Banana Bread

prep: 15 min.   bake: 1 hr., 5 min.   cool: 10 min.

The best-tasting banana bread comes from using overripe bananas. Yogurt adds a nice tang to this recipe.

2	cups self-rising flour
1	cup sugar
¼	cup toasted wheat germ
½	teaspoon baking soda
½	cup butter, melted
3	very ripe bananas, mashed (1½ cups)
2	large eggs, lightly beaten
¼	cup strawberry yogurt or vanilla yogurt
1½	teaspoons vanilla extract

Preheat oven to 350°. Grease and flour a 9- x 5-inch loaf pan; set aside.

Combine first 4 ingredients in a large bowl; make a well in center of mixture. Stir together melted butter, mashed banana, eggs, yogurt, and vanilla. Add to dry ingredients; stir just until moistened. Pour batter into prepared pan.

Bake at 350° for 1 hour and 5 minutes or until a wooden pick inserted in center comes out clean. Cover loosely with aluminum foil after 40 minutes if loaf begins to brown too quickly. Cool in pan on wire rack 10 minutes; remove from pan, and cool completely on wire rack. **Yield: 1 loaf.**

Note: For muffins, spoon batter into lightly greased or paper-lined muffin pans, filling three-fourths full. Bake at 350° for 19 to 21 minutes or until lightly browned. Remove from pans immediately. Let cool on wire racks. **Yield: 20 muffins.**

variations

Banana-Nut Bread: Add 1 cup chopped, toasted pecans to batter before baking.

Chocolate Chip-Banana Bread: Add 1 cup semisweet chocolate morsels to batter before baking.

Waffles Benedict

prep: 15 min.   stand: 5 min.   cook: 20 min.

You can substitute prosciutto, deli ham, or country ham for the pancetta. Sauté it briefly for extra flavor.

2 cups all-purpose baking mix*
1⅓ cups buttermilk
½ cup (2 ounces) shredded Parmesan cheese
2 tablespoons vegetable oil
9 large eggs
½ teaspoon white vinegar
1 (0.9-ounce) envelope hollandaise sauce mix*
1 tablespoon lemon juice
½ teaspoon fresh or ¼ teaspoon dried tarragon
8 thin pancetta slices (about ¼ pound)
Garnish: chopped fresh chives

Stir together baking mix, next 3 ingredients, and 1 egg in a medium bowl until blended. Let batter stand 5 minutes.

Meanwhile, add water to a depth of 3 inches in a large saucepan. Bring to a boil; reduce heat, and maintain a light simmer. Add vinegar. Working in 2 batches, break remaining 8 eggs, and slip into water, 1 at a time, as close as possible to surface. Simmer 3 to 5 minutes or to desired degree of doneness. Remove with a slotted spoon. Trim edges, if desired.

Cook batter in a preheated, lightly greased waffle iron according to manufacturer's directions until golden.

Prepare hollandaise sauce according to package directions, adding lemon juice and tarragon.

For each serving, stack 2 waffles, and top with 2 pancetta slices, 2 poached eggs, and desired amount of hollandaise sauce. Garnish, if desired. **Yield: 4 servings.**

*For testing purposes only, we used Bisquick Original Pancake and Baking Mix and Knorr Hollandaise Sauce Mix.

Pecan Streusel Coffee Cake

prep: 17 min.   bake: 45 min.

A buttery coffee crumb mixture makes a shortbreadlike crust for this easy snack cake. This is one of the best coffee cakes around.

2	cups all-purpose flour
2	teaspoons instant coffee granules
2	cups firmly packed light brown sugar
1	teaspoon ground cinnamon
½	teaspoon salt
½	cup chilled butter, cut into pieces
1	(8-ounce) carton sour cream
1	teaspoon baking soda
1	large egg, lightly beaten
1½	cups chopped pecans

Preheat oven to 350°. Combine flour and coffee granules in a large bowl. Add brown sugar, cinnamon, and salt; stir well. Cut in butter with a pastry blender until crumbly. Press half of crumb mixture into a greased 9-inch square pan; set aside.

Combine sour cream and baking soda, stirring well. Add to remaining crumb mixture, stirring just until dry ingredients are moistened. Add egg, stirring gently to combine. Pour sour cream mixture over crumb crust in pan; sprinkle with pecans.

Bake at 350° for 45 minutes. Cool and cut into squares. **Yield: 1 (9-inch) coffee cake.**

Almond French Toast

prep: 20 min.   stand: 5 min.   bake: 25 min.

Everyone needs an extravagant-tasting breakfast bread now and then. Bake this version in the oven instead of preparing it using the more involved stovetop method.

6	(1-inch-thick) French bread slices
4	large eggs
½	cup milk
1	tablespoon sugar
1	teaspoon almond extract
½	teaspoon vanilla extract
2	tablespoons almond liqueur (optional)
3	tablespoons butter
½	cup sliced almonds, toasted

Powdered sugar

Maple syrup, warmed

Arrange French bread slices in a 13- x 9-inch baking dish.

Whisk together eggs, next 4 ingredients, and, if desired, liqueur; pour over bread. Let stand 5 minutes, turning once. Cover and chill 8 hours, if desired.

Preheat oven to 400°. Melt butter at 400° in a 15- x 10-inch jelly-roll pan; add soaked bread slices.

Bake at 400° for 15 minutes; turn each slice, and bake 8 to 10 more minutes or until golden. Sprinkle with almonds and powdered sugar. Serve with maple syrup. **Yield: 3 servings.**

Caramel-Nut Pull-Apart Bread

prep: 12 min. bake: 35 min.

Gooey pull-apart bread goes over well at any breakfast table. This version is certainly no exception.

1 cup plus 2 tablespoons firmly packed
   brown sugar
1 cup chopped walnuts
¾ cup butter, melted
3 (12-ounce) cans refrigerated biscuits*
2 tablespoons cinnamon sugar

Preheat oven to 350°. Combine brown sugar and walnuts in a small bowl. Stir in butter. Spoon half of brown sugar mixture in bottom of a greased 12-cup Bundt pan.

Cut each biscuit in half (use kitchen scissors for quick cutting), and place in a large bowl. Sprinkle biscuits with cinnamon sugar; toss well to coat. Arrange half of biscuits over brown sugar mixture in Bundt pan. Spoon remaining brown sugar mixture over biscuits in pan; top with remaining biscuits.

Bake at 350° for 30 to 35 minutes or until browned. Turn out onto a serving platter immediately, spooning any remaining sauce over bread. Serve warm. **Yield: 12 servings.**

*For testing purposes only, we used Pillsbury Golden Layers Flaky Biscuits.

fresh from the garden

My Father's Voice

I can still hear my earliest food memory: the jangle of harness and my father's voice. On a cool spring day in East Texas in 1952, Dad, for the last time in our family, made a garden with a mule. "Gee" and "Haw" and "Come up," he commanded tersely, the mule's ears twitching like antennae, as man and animal broke up a field of broom sedge into long, straight rows ready for seed. My brother and I toddled alongside. "Stay out from behind the mule," Dad warned us repeatedly—the first words I can remember him speaking to me.

Dad watered and weeded for weeks on end. Then Mom prepared his peas, beans, and greens—boiled with pork and served with cornbread cooked in a skillet—as all women in our Southern family before her.

By the next spring the garden had returned to a broom sedge field that later gave way to a sandlot baseball diamond. In years ahead, our parents got busy with career and children, and turned from garden to grocer. My great aunt, who always grew more beans and tomatoes than she could "put up," let us pick from hers occasionally. One summer she even gave me a patch of my own to cultivate. Nothing, I learned, grows faster than weeds in peas.

These days we shop for vegetables from local gardens, cook them in ways other than boiling, and lighten up on the pork. They still taste of the mint of a distant spring day, however, and murmur with a long-ago language of man, mule, and earth.

—**Gary Ford, Senior Writer**

Homemade Applesauce

prep: 20 min.   cook: 20 min.

For the best taste and texture, use a variety of apples—such as Granny Smith, Golden Delicious, and Gala—when making applesauce and apple pie. Stir in a little chopped rosemary, and serve this applesauce as a side dish with pork chops or hash browns.

12   large apples, peeled and coarsely chopped
1   cup sugar
½   lemon, sliced

Cook all ingredients in a Dutch oven over medium heat, stirring often, 20 minutes or until apples are tender and juices are thickened. Remove and discard lemon slices. Serve applesauce warm; or let cool and store in an airtight container in the refrigerator for up to 1 week. **Yield: about 6 cups.**

variation

Spiced Applesauce: Substitute ½ cup firmly packed brown sugar and ½ cup granulated sugar for 1 cup sugar. Omit lemon slices, and add 1 teaspoon ground cinnamon and ¼ teaspoon ground cloves; prepare as directed.

Butter Beans With Cornbread Crust

prep: 15 min.   cook: 30 min.   bake: 20 min.

As an option, look for fresh speckled butter beans late in the summer at your local farmers market. Simmer the fresh beans a few minutes less.

4   cups chicken broth
2   (16-ounce) bags frozen butter beans
½   teaspoon salt
½   teaspoon pepper
1   large sweet onion, diced
1   poblano chile, diced
1   tablespoon olive oil
Cornbread Crust Batter

Bring first 4 ingredients to a boil in a large saucepan over medium-high heat. Reduce heat to low; cover and simmer 25 minutes or until beans are tender. Remove from heat.

Preheat oven to 425°. Sauté onion and chile in hot oil in a large skillet over medium-high heat 2 minutes; remove from heat, and stir into beans. Spoon bean mixture into a lightly greased 13- x 9-inch baking dish.

Spoon Cornbread Crust Batter over beans, spreading to edges of dish.

Bake at 425° for 20 minutes or until crust is golden brown. **Yield: 6 to 8 servings.**

Cornbread Crust Batter

prep: 5 min.

2   cups cornmeal mix
½   cup buttermilk
½   cup sour cream
2   large eggs, lightly beaten

Stir together all ingredients. Use in recipe above and bake as directed. **Yield: 3 cups.**

Broccoli-Carrot Salad

prep: 20 min.

Variations of this old-fashioned, slightly sweet broccoli salad have made many an appearance at church suppers across the South.

1½ pounds fresh broccoli
1   cup scraped, sliced, or shredded carrot
1   cup (4 ounces) shredded Cheddar cheese
1   cup raisins (optional)
½   cup mayonnaise
2   to 3 tablespoons sugar
2   teaspoons red wine vinegar
Lettuce leaves (optional)
8   bacon slices, cooked and crumbled

Remove broccoli leaves, and cut off tough ends of stalks; discard. Wash broccoli thoroughly, and cut into florets. Blanch broccoli in boiling water 10 seconds. Plunge into ice water to stop the cooking process; drain well.

Combine broccoli, carrot, cheese, and, if desired, raisins, tossing gently. Combine mayonnaise, sugar, and vinegar; stir well. Add mayonnaise dressing to broccoli mixture, and toss gently.

Spoon broccoli salad onto lettuce-lined salad plates, if desired, using a slotted spoon. Sprinkle with bacon, and serve immediately. **Yield: 8 servings.**

Fresh Corn Cakes

prep: 20 min.   cook: 7 min. per batch

Golden brown and hot off the griddle, these corn cakes are loaded with bits of melted mozzarella. (shown on page 86)

2½ cups fresh corn kernels (about 5 ears)
3   large eggs
¾   cup milk
3   tablespoons butter, melted
¾   cup all-purpose flour
¾   cup yellow or white cornmeal
1   (8-ounce) package fresh mozzarella
      cheese, shredded
2   tablespoons chopped fresh chives
1   teaspoon salt
1   teaspoon freshly ground pepper

Pulse first 4 ingredients in a food processor 3 or 4 times or just until corn is coarsely chopped.

Stir together flour and next 5 ingredients in a large bowl; stir in corn mixture just until dry ingredients are moistened.

Spoon ⅛ cup batter for each cake onto a hot, lightly greased griddle or large nonstick skillet to form 2-inch cakes (do not spread or flatten cakes). Cook cakes 3 to 4 minutes or until tops are covered with bubbles and edges look cooked. Turn and cook other sides 2 to 3 minutes. **Yield: about 3 dozen.**

Fried Corn

prep: 15 min.   cook: 27 min.

12   ears fresh corn
8   bacon slices
½   cup butter
2   to 4 tablespoons sugar
2   teaspoons salt
½   teaspoon pepper

Remove and discard husks and silks from corn. Cut off tips of corn kernels into a large bowl; scrape milk and remaining pulp from cob with a paring knife.

Cook bacon in a large skillet until crisp; remove bacon, reserving 3 tablespoons drippings in skillet. Crumble bacon.

Cook corn, butter, and remaining 3 ingredients in bacon drippings over medium heat 20 minutes or until corn is lightly browned, stirring often. Spoon corn into a serving dish; sprinkle with bacon. **Yield: 12 servings.**

Corn Pudding

prep: 18 min.   bake: 47 min.   stand: 5 min.

Creamed corn baked in custard is a traditional Southern dish worth preserving.

9   ears fresh corn
4   large eggs, beaten
½   cup half-and-half
1½ teaspoons baking powder
⅓   cup butter
2   tablespoons sugar
2   tablespoons all-purpose flour
1   tablespoon butter, melted
⅛   teaspoon freshly ground pepper

Remove and discard husks and silks from corn. Cut off tips of corn kernels into a bowl, and scrape milk and remaining pulp from cob with a paring knife to measure 3 to 4 cups total. Set corn aside.

Combine eggs, half-and-half, and baking powder, stirring well with a wire whisk.
Preheat oven to 350°. Melt ⅓ cup butter in a large saucepan over low heat; add sugar and flour, stirring until smooth. Remove from heat; gradually add egg mixture, whisking constantly until smooth. Stir in corn.
Pour corn mixture into a greased 1- or 1½-quart baking dish.
Bake, uncovered, at 350° for 40 to 45 minutes or until pudding is set. Drizzle pudding with 1 tablespoon butter; sprinkle with pepper.
Broil 5½ inches from heat 2 minutes or until golden. Let stand 5 minutes before serving.
Yield: 6 to 8 servings.

The British don't like corn. They say it's animal feed. Well, if that's true, saddle me up and enter me in the Kentucky Derby because sweet Silver Queen corn is my manna from heaven. There are not enough hot, buttered Silver Queen ears on Earth to sate my desire. Fill a barn with them, and I'll finish them off by noon.

—Steve Bender, Senior Writer

Cucumber Sandwiches

prep: 10 min.

Cold cucumber sandwiches are one of the ultimate feel-good foods that strike a chord with ladies of all ages.

1 large cucumber, peeled, seeded, and grated
1 (8-ounce) package cream cheese, softened
1 tablespoon mayonnaise
1 small shallot, minced
¼ teaspoon seasoned salt
1 (16-ounce) loaf sandwich bread
Garnish: cucumber slices

Drain cucumber well, pressing between layers of paper towels.

Stir together cucumber and next 4 ingredients. Spread mixture over half of bread slices. Top with remaining bread slices.

Trim crusts from sandwiches, and cut in half diagonally. Garnish, if desired. Store sandwiches in an airtight container in refrigerator. **Yield: 16 sandwiches.**

When my mother died unexpectedly, food began arriving almost immediately, in true Southern tradition. I had deep gratitude for this outpouring of love but, unfortunately, no appetite. However, the day of the funeral, one of my mother's friends, Jewel Robbins, brought a platter of beautiful little cold cucumber sandwiches. I'll never forget how good they tasted and how good they made me feel—or how many I ate.

—Carolyn Pedison, *Southern Living* Reader

Grits and Greens

prep: 15 min.   cook: 1 hr.

Two classic Southern foods come together in this old-fashioned yet trendy recipe. Stir them together, or spoon them side by side on each plate. And don't forget the ham garnish; sauté it briefly for the best flavor.

1   cup whipping cream
4   cups chicken broth, divided
1   cup uncooked stone-ground grits
¼   to ½ cup milk or chicken broth (optional)
1   pound fresh collard greens
¼   cup butter
1   to 1½ cups (4 to 6 ounces) freshly grated
      Parmesan cheese
¼   to ½ teaspoon freshly ground pepper
Garnish: cubed cooked ham or chopped cooked
      bacon

Combine whipping cream and 3 cups chicken broth in a large saucepan. Bring to a boil, and gradually stir in grits.

Cook over medium heat until mixture returns to a boil; cover, reduce heat, and simmer 25 to 30 minutes, stirring often. Gradually add milk or more chicken broth, if necessary, for desired consistency.

Remove and discard stems and any discolored spots from greens. Wash greens thoroughly; drain and cut into ½-inch strips.

Combine greens and remaining 1 cup chicken broth in a large skillet; bring to a boil. Cover, reduce heat, and simmer 10 to 20 minutes or until greens are tender.

Add butter, cheese, and pepper to grits, stirring until butter and cheese are melted. Stir in greens, if desired; cook just until thoroughly heated. Or serve grits and greens side by side on each plate. Garnish, if desired. **Yield: 6 to 8 servings.**

Crunchy Fried Okra

prep: 20 min.   cook: 2 min. per batch

Whole okra, halved lengthwise, gives a fun twist to this fried favorite.

1½ cups buttermilk
1   large egg
2   cups saltine cracker crumbs (2 sleeves)
1½ cups all-purpose flour
1   teaspoon salt
1   pound fresh okra, cut in half lengthwise
Peanut oil
Salt (optional)

Stir together buttermilk and egg. Combine cracker crumbs, flour, and salt. Dip okra pieces in buttermilk mixture; dredge in cracker crumb mixture.

Pour oil to a depth of 2 inches into a Dutch oven or cast-iron skillet; heat to 375°. Fry okra, in 3 batches, 2 minutes or until golden, turning once. Drain on paper towels. Sprinkle lightly with salt, if desired. **Yield: 4 to 6 servings.**

Fourth of July Tomatoes

For most people July Fourth means picnics and fireworks. To me it means tomatoes. Big, red, juicy tomatoes with just the right balance of tart, acid flavor and a silky-smooth texture.

My father loved to garden. He was especially proud of his tomatoes, which he started from seed early each spring. He judged his gardening skills by whether he had a ripe tomato by the Fourth of July. The size of the tomato didn't matter as long as it was ripe and ready to eat.

From mid-June until July Fourth each day's conversation included a prediction on whether he'd have a ripe tomato by the Fourth. Once this goal was achieved, and from July fifth until the first killing frost, tomatoes were a part of every meal. Whether simply sliced or cut into wedges and sprinkled with salt and pepper, fried, stewed, stuffed, or served between mayonnaise-slathered slices of white bread, tomatoes were a staple. Today, although I can buy tomatoes year-round, there's still a little part of me that thinks tomato season doesn't really begin until that first tomato eaten on the Fourth of July.

—Kathy Eakin, Executive Editor, Books

Okra and Tomatoes

prep: 25 min.   cook: 20 min.

Juicy, summer-ripe tomatoes make this dish shine. You can use a large can of San Marzano tomatoes, chopped, as an out-of-season option.

4	bacon slices
1	large sweet onion, chopped
3	large tomatoes, chopped
1	pound fresh okra, chopped
1	teaspoon salt
1	teaspoon pepper
1	garlic clove, minced

Hot cooked rice

Cook bacon in a large skillet or Dutch oven over medium heat until crisp. Remove and crumble bacon; reserve 2 tablespoons drippings in skillet.

Sauté onion in hot drippings over medium-high heat 5 minutes or until tender. Stir in tomatoes and next 4 ingredients. Reduce heat, and cook, stirring often, 10 minutes or until okra is tender. Serve over rice, and sprinkle with bacon. **Yield: 8 servings.**

Green Peas With Crispy Bacon

prep: 20 min.   cook: 17 min.

Mint and orange brighten the flavor of this simple side dish. Early in the season, while you can, use fresh peas. Boy, are they ever good.

4	bacon slices
2	shallots, sliced
1	teaspoon orange zest
1	cup fresh orange juice
1	teaspoon pepper
½	teaspoon salt
2	(16-ounce) bags frozen sweet green peas, thawed*
2	to 3 tablespoons chopped fresh mint
1	tablespoon butter

Cook bacon in a large skillet over medium heat until crisp. Remove and crumble bacon; reserve 2 teaspoons drippings in skillet.

Sauté shallots in hot drippings over medium-high heat 2 minutes or until tender. Stir in orange zest, orange juice, pepper, and salt. Cook, stirring occasionally, 5 minutes or until reduced by half. Add peas, and cook 5 minutes; stir in mint and butter.

Transfer peas to a serving dish, and sprinkle with crumbled bacon. **Yield: 12 servings.**

*6 cups shelled fresh sweet green peas may be substituted. Cook peas in boiling water to cover 5 minutes; drain and proceed with recipe as directed.

Summer Squash Casserole

prep: 25 min.   cook: 5 min.   bake: 35 min.   stand: 10 min.

There's just something about a classic vegetable casserole that's impossible to resist. Even picky eaters go back for second helpings.

1½   pounds yellow squash
1   pound zucchini
1   small sweet onion, chopped
2½   teaspoons salt, divided
1   cup grated carrots
1   (10¾-ounce) can cream of chicken soup
1   (8-ounce) container sour cream
1   (8-ounce) can water chestnuts, drained and chopped
1   (8-ounce) bag herb-seasoned stuffing*
½   cup butter, melted

Preheat oven to 350°. Cut squash and zucchini into ¼-inch-thick slices; place in a Dutch oven. Add chopped onion, 2 teaspoons salt, and water to cover. Bring to a boil over medium-high heat, and cook 5 minutes; drain well.

Stir together grated carrots, next 3 ingredients, and remaining ½ teaspoon salt in a large bowl; fold in squash mixture. Stir together stuffing and melted butter; spoon half of stuffing mixture into bottom of a lightly greased 13- x 9-inch baking dish. Spoon squash mixture over stuffing mixture, and top with remaining stuffing mixture.

Bake at 350° for 30 to 35 minutes or until bubbly and golden brown, shielding with aluminum foil after 20 to 25 minutes to prevent excessive browning, if necessary. Let stand 10 minutes before serving. **Yield: 8 servings.**

*For testing purposes only, we used Pepperidge Farm Herb Seasoned Stuffing.

Crumb-Topped Spinach Casserole

prep: 13 min.   cook: 8 min.   bake: 35 min.

This quick, cheesy side, with its crunchy browned topping, can be ready to bake in just over the time it takes to preheat the oven. This recipe is *the one* to introduce kids to spinach.

2   tablespoons butter
1   medium onion, chopped
2   garlic cloves, minced
4   (10-ounce) packages frozen chopped spinach, thawed
1   (8-ounce) package cream cheese, softened
2   tablespoons all-purpose flour
2   large eggs
½   teaspoon salt
¼   teaspoon pepper
1   cup milk
1   (8-ounce) package shredded Cheddar cheese
1   cup Italian-seasoned Japanese breadcrumbs (panko) or homemade breadcrumbs
3   to 4 tablespoons butter, melted

Preheat oven to 350°. Melt 2 tablespoons butter in a large nonstick skillet over medium heat. Add onion and garlic, and sauté 8 minutes or until tender.

Meanwhile, drain spinach well, pressing between paper towels to remove excess moisture.

Stir together cream cheese and flour in a large bowl until smooth. Whisk in eggs, salt, and pepper. Gradually whisk in milk until blended. Add sautéed onion, spinach, and Cheddar cheese, stirring until blended. Spoon into a lightly greased 11- x 7-inch baking dish.

Combine breadcrumbs and 3 to 4 tablespoons butter in a small bowl; toss well. Sprinkle over casserole.

Bake, uncovered, at 350° for 30 to 35 minutes or until thoroughly heated and breadcrumbs are browned. **Yield: 8 to 10 servings.**

Note: To make individual spinach casseroles, spoon spinach mixture into 8 (8-ounce) lightly greased ramekins; top each with buttered breadcrumbs. Bake, uncovered, at 375° for 25 to 30 minutes or until browned. (We found that a slightly higher temperature produced better results for individual casseroles.)

Summer of the Perfect Tomato

I honestly don't even know the year, but the events revisit me every time—yes, *every* time—I meet up with a tomato of the very red, very slurpy, almost husky-with-flavor variety. Travel back to that tasty time with me: Ann Griffith, my wonderful mother and a gifted newspaper columnist, wrote a piece voicing concern that the old-fashioned tomato had given way to hothouse wannabes (those pale round things that taste like pink-tinted cardboard).

Defensive readers loaded bushel baskets, paper bags, and gunny sacks and drove to the headquarters of the *Charleston Daily Mail,* armed with evidence. Very red, very slurpy, definitely husky-with-flavor evidence that my mother brought home daily throughout the entire growing season. We ate them like apples, shaking white granules from little blue Morton saltshakers. Sometimes we sprinkled sugar instead. Mom cooked tomatoes into every recipe available (where was this cookbook back then?!). She did write a follow-up column celebrating the healthy—and oh-so-prolific—State of the Tomato.

A wonderful recent discovery now makes me count the days to summer's start: My chef friend Chris Hastings at Hot and Hot Fish Club, in Birmingham, Alabama, serves a Tomato Salad with applewood-smoked bacon, fresh peas, corn, fried okra, and chive aïoli. It's a long name for pure heaven. Now my son—exactly the age I was back then—adores the local appetizer. And I suspect it's the beginning of *his* Summer of the Perfect Tomato memories. How just, how right, how … slurpy wonderful.

—Carolanne Griffith Roberts, Travel Editor

Floyd's Favorite Tomato Sandwich

prep: 10 min.   chill: 8 hr.

Editor in Chief John Floyd recommends large heirloom beefsteak varieties, such as Red Brandywine and Aunt Ginny's Purple, which are not only perfect for slicing but also have a classic rich and juicy tomato flavor.

1	large ripe tomato, peeled
1	large onion
3	tablespoons mayonnaise
1	tablespoon mustard
16	sandwich bread slices
⅛	teaspoon salt
⅛	teaspoon pepper

Cut tomato and onion into 8 (¼-inch-thick) slices.

Layer slices in a shallow dish; cover and chill 8 hours. Discard onion slices, or reserve for other uses.

Stir together mayonnaise and mustard; spread on 1 side of each bread slice. Place 1 tomato slice on each of 8 bread slices; sprinkle lightly with salt and pepper. Top with remaining bread slices. Cover and chill up to 2 days, if desired.

Yield: 8 sandwiches.

Feta-Stuffed Tomatoes

prep: 15 min.   bake: 15 min.

4   large tomatoes
4   ounces crumbled feta cheese
¼   cup fine, dry breadcrumbs
2   tablespoons chopped green onions
2   tablespoons chopped fresh
    flat-leaf parsley
2   tablespoons olive oil
¼   teaspoon salt
¼   teaspoon pepper
Garnish: fresh flat-leaf parsley

Preheat oven to 350°. Cut tomatoes in half horizontally. Scoop out pulp from each tomato half, leaving shells intact; discard seeds, and coarsely chop pulp.

Stir together pulp, feta cheese, and next 6 ingredients in a bowl. Spoon mixture into tomato shells, and place in a 13- x 9-inch baking dish.

Bake at 350° for 15 minutes. Garnish, if desired.
Yield: 8 servings.

Fried Green Tomatoes

prep: 15 min.   cook: 6 min. per batch

Dipped first in buttermilk and then in a flour-and-cornmeal coating before frying, these tomatoes come out hot, crisp, and juicy.

4	large green tomatoes
1½	cups buttermilk
1	tablespoon salt
1	teaspoon pepper
1	cup all-purpose flour
1	cup self-rising cornmeal
3	cups vegetable oil
Salt to taste	

Cut tomatoes into ¼- to ⅓-inch-thick slices; place in a shallow dish. Pour buttermilk over tomatoes. Sprinkle with salt and pepper.

Combine flour and cornmeal in a shallow dish or pieplate. Dredge tomato slices in flour mixture.

Fry tomatoes, in batches, in hot oil in a large cast-iron skillet over medium heat 3 minutes on each side or until golden. Drain tomatoes on paper towels. Sprinkle with salt to taste.
Yield: 6 to 8 servings.

A Simple Salad

My mother never put a meal on the table without serving a salad of iceberg lettuce and Italian dressing from a silver bowl. What the salad accompanied wouldn't impress foodies, but in hindsight I see that she pulled off quite a feat. My brother and I sat at the table every night. We unfolded square paper napkins in our laps and used my mother's silverware, an unpretentious pattern that felt good and solid in my hand.

I remember only a few dishes Mom ever made: lemon pepper chicken and rice, macaroni and cheese with tuna, and the artichoke.

That beautiful, weird leafy plant made dinner into an occasion. My mother rarely cooked artichokes because they were expensive and she was a single mother on a budget. When she did, she would buy only one, and the three of us would share it, dipping the meaty ends into mayonnaise, discarding the leaves in a central bowl, and splitting the succulent heart after the leaves were gone.

My evening meals are now shaped by memories of my lovely mother, of dinner-table laughter, of always drinking a glass of cold milk—never a soda—and of savoring a simple salad.

My two children and I always sit at the table. We use cloth napkins rather than paper, but we laugh as much as that threesome from my childhood. I attempt new recipes from dog-eared magazine pages, but Kate and Jacob are happiest when I serve chicken and rice. And sometimes I make dinner an occasion with a weird leafy artichoke perfect for sharing.

—Amy Bickers Mercer, Associate Home Editor

Lettuce Wedge Salad

prep: 30 min.   cook: 15 min.

What's old is new again—and with a certain tasty charm. Who can resist a simple iceberg wedge, especially when it's icy cold?

4   to 6 bacon slices
1   medium onion, sliced
1   cup buttermilk
½   cup sour cream
1   (1-ounce) envelope Ranch-style dressing mix
¼   cup chopped fresh basil
2   garlic cloves
1   large head iceberg lettuce, cut into 4 wedges
Shredded basil (optional)

Cook bacon in a large skillet over medium heat until crisp; remove bacon, and drain on paper towels, reserving 1 tablespoon drippings in skillet. Crumble bacon, and set aside.

Sauté onion in hot drippings in skillet over medium heat 10 minutes or until tender and lightly browned. Remove from heat; cool.
Process onion, buttermilk, and next 4 ingredients in a blender or food processor until smooth, stopping to scrape down sides.
Top each lettuce wedge with dressing; sprinkle with bacon, and top with shredded basil, if desired. **Yield: 4 servings.**

Note: You can make the dressing ahead and store it in the refrigerator. The chilled dressing will have a thicker consistency.

Watermelon Rind Pickles

prep: 1 hr., 30 min.   cook: 1 hr., 30 min.   stand: 16 hr.

Don't toss that watermelon rind! Here's a novel condiment that's both spicy and sweet. These pickles belong on a picnic plate next to peas, fried chicken, and a hot biscuit.

1	large watermelon (about 7 pounds)
¾	cup salt
2	quarts ice cubes
1	tablespoon whole cloves
1	tablespoon whole allspice
9	cups sugar
3	cups white vinegar (5% acidity)
1	lemon, thinly sliced
5	(3-inch) cinnamon sticks

Quarter watermelon; remove all pink flesh (if you haven't already eaten it). Peel green skin from watermelon rind. Cut enough rind into 1-inch cubes to yield 12 cups, and place cubed rind in a large container. Discard any remaining rind.

Stir together salt and 3 quarts water; pour over rind. Add ice; cover and let stand 8 hours. Rinse well, and drain.

Cook rind in water to cover in a Dutch oven over high heat 10 minutes or until tender. Drain and place rind in large container.

Place cloves and allspice on a 3-inch square of cheesecloth; tie with string.

Stir together sugar, vinegar, and 3 cups water in Dutch oven; add spice bag, and bring to a boil. Boil 5 minutes, and pour over rind in large container. Stir in lemon slices. Cover and let stand 8 hours.

Bring rind and syrup mixture to a boil in a Dutch oven; reduce heat, and simmer, stirring occasionally, 1 hour. Discard spice bag.

Pack rind mixture into hot jars, filling ½ inch from top. Add 1 cinnamon stick to each jar. Remove air bubbles; wipe jar rims. Cover at once with metal lids, and screw on bands.

Process in a boiling-water bath 10 minutes. **Yield: 5 (12-ounce) jars.**

casseroles & beyond

bake at
350°
45 to

Comfort To Go

Like a wave of giblet gravy (or was it PTA Punch?), the memories came flooding back. I was sitting on the floor of the parents' living room, watching a cousin serve some chocolate-covered pecans that my aunt had made.

I glanced up just in time to see a familiar flash of red. There, on the bottom of the candy plate, were my aunt's initials neatly painted in crimson nail polish. And I could just hear my mother saying, "We've got to carry food."

Like most of their contemporaries, Mother and my aunts have carried so much food to so many neighbors that they have had to brand their dishes. Otherwise, they'd never find them again.

Somebody's sick? Send a Dutch oven full of homemade soup. An elderly deacon isn't up to the fellowship? Carry him a heaping plate (and double up on the chocolate cake—he's got a sweet tooth, bless his heart). A family lost a loved one? Better take two fried chickens, some deviled eggs, a pot of black-eyed peas, and a gallon of sweet tea. Oh, and maybe a package of those little dinner rolls. You can just warm those in the microwave.

When I was very small, Mother couldn't bring herself to write directly on her platters and bowls. Instead, she would write her name on a strip of masking tape and stick it to the bottom of the dish. But after much lost tape in soapy dishwater and a few misplaced pie plates, she finally resorted to using nail polish.

Of course when those dishes are filled with food, nobody back home needs a bright red initial to know who cooked what. We can spot Mother's fried chicken a mile away. Or Aunt Rosie's cobbler. Or Billie Darby's anything. There's always a long line next to

continued

Billie's cakes at the fellowship table. She is rumored to make everything from scratch.

Few things put me to sleep quicker than a baby shower or bridal tea, but even I will break down and attend one at Billie's house because I know the refreshments will be well worth the price of admission. I don't mind standing around in high heels, ooing and aahing over diaper bags or china patterns, if I know all the while there are home-made cheese straws at the end of the rainbow.

For women like Billie, Mother, and my aunts, preparing food for others truly is a labor of love. They do it not because they like spending all their time in the kitchen, but because they want to say to a neighbor in good times or bad, "We love you. You're part of us. You can count on us." It's one of the simplest, purest, most unselfish forms of friendship and compassion you'll find.

And as I've watched these women brand their dishes, grate their coconut, sprinkle breadcrumbs over their chicken casseroles, and go through miles and miles of tin foil and plastic wrap, I've reached one conclusion: If your name is on your dishes, then it's probably written in The Book, too.

—**Valerie Fraser Luesse, Creative Development Director**

Poppy Seed-Chicken Casserole

prep: 12 min.   bake: 30 min.   stand: 10 min.

This timeless casserole might just be what put poppy seeds on the map. We gave this version a healthy spin with whole wheat crackers.

3   to 4 cups chopped cooked chicken or turkey
1   (10¾-ounce) can cream of chicken and mushroom soup
1   (16-ounce) container sour cream or light sour cream
1½   cups (6 ounces) shredded sharp Cheddar cheese
3   tablespoons poppy seeds
1   sleeve whole wheat round buttery crackers, crushed
¼   cup butter, melted

Preheat oven to 350°. Combine first 5 ingredients in a large bowl; stir well. Spoon into a lightly greased 11- x 7-inch baking dish. Top with crushed crackers. Drizzle with melted butter.

Bake, uncovered, at 350° for 25 to 30 minutes or until bubbly. Let stand 10 minutes before serving. **Yield: 6 servings.**

Note: You can crush the crackers while they're still in the sleeve. Gently crush with your hands; then open crackers at one end, and sprinkle right onto the casserole.

Long Live the Casserole

After the birth of our first child, my family was overwhelmed by the generosity of friends bringing meals. One vivid memory still brings a chuckle: Three wonderful friends each brought their rendition of Poppy Seed-Chicken Casserole to our house within the same week. With each ring of the doorbell, I smiled anew wholeheartedly and accepted the dish and all that it stood for: tradition, friendship, and the notion that you just can't beat a good chicken casserole.

—Julie Gunter, Food Editor

Chicken Tetrazzini

prep: 20 min.   bake: 35 min.

Tetrazzini is a house-favorite cheese-and-chicken entrée. This version serves plenty of people.

1	(16-ounce) package vermicelli
½	cup chicken broth
4	cups chopped cooked chicken
1	(10¾-ounce) can cream of mushroom soup
1	(10¾-ounce) can cream of chicken soup
1	(10¾-ounce) can cream of celery soup
1	(8-ounce) container sour cream
1	(6-ounce) jar sliced mushrooms, drained
½	cup (2 ounces) shredded Parmesan cheese
1	teaspoon pepper
½	teaspoon salt
2	cups (8 ounces) shredded Cheddar cheese

Cook vermicelli according to package directions; drain. Return to pot, and toss with chicken broth.

Preheat oven to 350°. Stir together chopped cooked chicken and next 8 ingredients in a large bowl; add vermicelli, and toss well. Spoon chicken mixture into 2 lightly greased 11- x 7-inch baking dishes. Sprinkle with Cheddar cheese.

Bake, covered, at 350° for 30 minutes; uncover and bake 5 more minutes or until cheese is bubbly. **Yield: 12 servings.**

Note: Freeze unbaked casserole up to 1 month, if desired. Thaw casserole overnight in refrigerator. Let stand 30 minutes at room temperature, and bake as directed.

Chicken-and-Rice Casserole

prep: 20 min. bake: 25 min.

Use a rotisserie chicken for this family-friendly casserole. The potato chip topping promises to be a hit.

2	tablespoons butter
1	medium onion, chopped
1	(8.8-ounce) package microwaveable rice of choice
3	cups chopped cooked chicken
1½	cups frozen petite peas
1½	cups (6 ounces) shredded sharp Cheddar cheese
1	cup mayonnaise
1	(10¾-ounce) can cream of chicken soup
1	(8-ounce) can sliced water chestnuts, drained
1	(4-ounce) jar sliced pimientos, drained
3	cups coarsely crushed ridged potato chips

Preheat oven to 350°. Melt butter in a skillet over medium heat. Add onion, and sauté 5 minutes or until tender.

Cook rice in microwave according to package directions. Combine sautéed onion, rice, chicken, and next 6 ingredients in a large bowl; toss gently. Spoon mixture into a lightly greased 13- x 9-inch baking dish. Top with coarsely crushed potato chips.

Bake, uncovered, at 350° for 20 to 25 minutes or until bubbly. **Yield: 8 servings.**

Note: To make casserole ahead, prepare and spoon casserole into baking dish, leaving off crushed chips. Cover and refrigerate up to 24 hours. Uncover and add crushed chips before baking.

Leslie's Favorite Chicken-and-Wild Rice Casserole

prep: 30 min.   cook: 10 min.   bake: 40 min.

This is one of those creamy, cheesy chicken casseroles. Perfect for a big family get-together, it feeds a crowd. You can make and freeze the casserole ahead, or make two smaller casseroles.

2	(6.2-ounce) packages fast-cooking long-grain and wild rice mix
¼	cup butter
4	celery ribs, chopped
2	medium onions, chopped
2	(8-ounce) cans sliced water chestnuts, drained
5	cups chopped cooked chicken
4	cups (16 ounces) shredded Cheddar cheese, divided
2	(10¾-ounce) cans cream of mushroom soup
2	(8-ounce) containers sour cream
1	cup milk
½	teaspoon salt
½	teaspoon pepper
2	cups soft breadcrumbs (homemade)
1	(2.25-ounce) package sliced almonds, toasted

Preheat oven to 350°. Prepare rice mixes according to package directions.

Melt butter in a large skillet over medium heat; add celery and onions. Sauté 10 minutes or until tender. Stir in rice, water chestnuts, chicken, 3 cups cheese, and next 5 ingredients.

Spoon mixture into a lightly greased 4-quart baking dish or lasagna pan. Top casserole with breadcrumbs.

Bake at 350° for 35 minutes. Sprinkle with remaining 1 cup cheese and almonds; bake 5 more minutes. **Yield: 10 to 12 servings.**

Note: You can divide this casserole evenly between 2 (13- x 9-inch) baking dishes. They'll just be slightly shallow as opposed to brimming over. Bake as directed above, or freeze casseroles up to 1 month. Remove from freezer, and let stand at room temperature 1 hour. Bake, covered, at 350° for 30 minutes. Uncover casseroles, and bake 55 more minutes. Sprinkle with remaining 1 cup cheese and almonds, and bake 5 more minutes.

Quick-and-Easy King Ranch Chicken Casserole

prep: 30 min.   cook: 17 min.   bake: 55 min.   stand: 10 min.

2   tablespoons butter

1   medium onion, chopped

1   medium-size green bell pepper, chopped

1   garlic clove, pressed

¾   cup chicken broth

1   (10¾-ounce) can cream of mushroom soup

1   (10¾-ounce) can cream of chicken soup

2   (10-ounce) cans diced tomatoes and green chiles, drained

1   teaspoon dried oregano

1   teaspoon ground cumin

1   teaspoon Mexican-style or other chili powder

1   (2-pound) skinned, boned, and shredded deli-roasted chicken

3   cups (12 ounces) shredded sharp Cheddar cheese

3   cups coarsely crumbled lime-flavored white corn tortilla chips

Preheat oven to 350°. Melt butter in a large skillet over medium-high heat. Add onion, and sauté 5 minutes or until tender. Add bell pepper and garlic, and sauté 3 to 4 minutes. Stir in chicken broth, cream of mushroom soup, and next 5 ingredients. Cook, stirring occasionally, 8 minutes.

Layer half of shredded chicken in a lightly greased 13- x 9-inch baking dish. Top with half of soup mixture and 1 cup Cheddar cheese. Cover with half of crumbled tortilla chips. Repeat layers once. Top with remaining 1 cup cheese.

Bake at 350° for 55 minutes or until bubbly. Let stand 10 minutes before serving. **Yield: 8 to 10 servings.**

Cassoulet

prep: 15 min.   stand: 1 hr.   cook: 1 hr., 25 min.   bake: 1 hr., 35 min.

A cassoulet is a hearty peasant dish with roots in the southwest of France. This version is a bit streamlined (or Americanized) but still boasts a garlicky breadcrumb top and plenty of beans and herb flavor. Several crusty baguettes are in order for this meal.

2	cups dried Great Northern beans
2	tablespoons olive oil
1	pound boneless center-cut pork chops
8	slices thick-cut smoked bacon, chopped
2	medium onions, chopped
8	garlic cloves, halved
1	tablespoon chopped fresh thyme
¼	cup tomato paste
8	cups chicken broth
1	cup dry white wine
1	cup fresh breadcrumbs
	(from a French baguette)
2	tablespoons butter, melted
1	garlic clove, minced

Sort and rinse beans; combine beans and 8 cups water in a Dutch oven. Bring to a boil; cover, reduce heat, and simmer 2 minutes. Remove from heat. Let stand 1 hour; drain.

Heat oil in a Dutch oven over medium-high heat; add pork chops. Cook 4 minutes on each side or until browned. Remove pork from Dutch oven, reserving drippings in pan. Cool pork slightly, and chop. Cover and refrigerate.

Cook bacon in reserved pork drippings in Dutch oven until crisp. Add onions, and cook 5 minutes or until tender. Add beans, halved garlic cloves, and next 3 ingredients. Bring to a boil; cover, reduce heat, and simmer 1 hour or until beans are almost tender. Drain; reserve bean mixture and 3 cups broth separately.

Preheat oven to 350°. Return bean mixture to Dutch oven or other ovenproof cookware; add pork, reserved 3 cups broth, and wine. Cover and bake at 350° for 1 hour and 15 minutes or until most of liquid has been absorbed.

Toss together breadcrumbs, butter, and minced garlic. Sprinkle over bean mixture; bake, uncovered, 20 minutes or until crumbs are golden. **Yield: 8 cups.**

Creole Jambalaya

prep: 25 min.   cook: 1 hr.

Jambalaya is traditionally made in one pot, with meat, veggies, and finally rice added near the end of cooking. This Creole version, which is also referred to as Red Jambalaya, sports a tomato base. On the other hand, Cajun Jambalaya is brown, made with stock and seasonings, and has no tomato products. Preferences aside, this historic entrée remains a notable stick-to-your-ribs comfort dish.

2	tablespoons butter
1	large onion, chopped
1	green bell pepper, chopped
8	green onions, chopped
2	celery ribs, chopped
3	cups cubed cooked ham (1 pound)
1	pound Cajun-flavored or smoked sausage, sliced
1	(8-ounce) can tomato sauce
½	teaspoon salt
½	teaspoon ground black pepper
¼	teaspoon ground red pepper
5	cups cooked rice

Melt butter in a large skillet over medium heat. Add onion and next 3 ingredients; sauté until tender. Add ham, sausage, and next 4 ingredients. Cook, stirring occasionally, 20 minutes. **Stir** in rice; cover and cook, stirring occasionally, 30 minutes over low heat. **Yield: 8 servings.**

Scalloped Potatoes With Ham

prep: 20 min.   bake: 1 hr., 10 min.   stand: 10 min.

Nutty Gruyère cheese and sweet potatoes give this dish fresh appeal.

1   medium onion, chopped

1   tablespoon vegetable oil

3   garlic cloves, finely chopped

2   sweet potatoes, peeled and cut
into ¼-inch slices (about 1½ pounds)

2   baking potatoes, peeled and cut
into ¼-inch slices (about 1½ pounds)

½   cup all-purpose flour

1   teaspoon salt

¼   teaspoon pepper

2   cups chopped cooked ham

2   cups (8 ounces) shredded Gruyère cheese,
divided

1¾ cups whipping cream

2   tablespoons butter, cut into pieces

Sauté onion in oil over medium-high heat 5 minutes or until tender. Add garlic; cook 30 seconds. Remove from heat, and set aside. Place potatoes in a large bowl.

Preheat oven to 400°. Combine flour, salt, and pepper; sprinkle over potatoes, tossing to coat. Arrange half of potato mixture in a greased 13- x 9-inch baking dish or 3-quart gratin dish. Top with onion, ham, and 1 cup cheese. Top with remaining potato mixture. Pour cream over potato mixture. Dot with butter, and cover with aluminum foil.

Bake at 400° for 50 minutes. Uncover, top with remaining 1 cup cheese, and bake 20 more minutes or until potatoes are tender and cheese is browned. Let stand 10 minutes before serving.

Yield: 6 servings.

The Southern Way

Throughout the construction of our new home, friends and their food gifts fueled us onward. Couples dropped by on hot weekend afternoons—tall, cold drinks or ice-cream cones in hand. Our future next-door neighbors forced us to take breaks by occasionally calling us over to join them for a relaxing dinner. And when we moved and our kitchen was trapped in cardboard boxes, we didn't have to worry about nourishment for almost a week.

The Southern philosophy is right: Home-cooked meals—and the support behind them—do make things easier. And don't be surprised if your serving dishes are returned filled with treats for *you* to enjoy.

—Dana Adkins Campbell, Food Editor, 1963–2003

Fabulous Tuna-Noodle Casserole

prep: 18 min.   cook: 15 min.   bake: 40 min.

¼   cup butter
1   large red bell pepper, chopped
1   cup chopped onion
1   (8-ounce) package sliced fresh mushrooms
⅓   cup all-purpose flour
3   cups milk
3   cups (12 ounces) shredded Cheddar cheese
¾   teaspoon salt
½   teaspoon pepper
1   (12-ounce) can solid white tuna in spring water, drained and flaked
1   (6-ounce) can solid white tuna in spring water, drained and flaked
1   (12-ounce) package egg noodles, cooked
¼   cup chopped fresh flat-leaf parsley
1½   cups homemade breadcrumbs
⅓   cup butter, melted

Preheat oven to 375°. Melt ¼ cup butter in a large skillet over medium-high heat; add bell pepper, onion, and mushrooms, and sauté 5 minutes or until tender. Remove from skillet.
Whisk together flour and milk until smooth; add to skillet. Cook over medium heat, stirring constantly, 10 minutes or until thickened. Remove from heat; add cheese, salt, and pepper, stirring until cheese is melted.
Stir in tuna, noodles, and parsley; stir in sautéed vegetables. Spoon into a lightly greased 13- x 9-inch baking dish.
Bake, covered, at 375° for 25 minutes. Stir together breadcrumbs and ⅓ cup melted butter; sprinkle over casserole, and bake, uncovered, 15 more minutes or until golden.
Yield: 6 to 8 servings.

Linguine Carbonara

prep: 15 min.   cook: 14 min.

A simple pasta dish is hard to top. Add another fresh herb, such as basil, if it's on hand.

½   pound bacon, cut into 1-inch pieces
¼   cup olive oil
1   medium onion, chopped
1   cup chopped fresh flat-leaf parsley
4   ounces fontina cheese, cut into small pieces
3   ounces prosciutto, cut into strips
16   ounces uncooked linguine
4   egg yolks, lightly beaten
¾   cup half-and-half or whipping cream, heated
1   teaspoon salt
Freshly ground pepper to taste
1   cup freshly grated Parmesan cheese, divided

Cook bacon in a large skillet over medium heat until crisp. Drain on paper towels. Pour off drippings; add oil and onion to skillet, and sauté 5 minutes or until onion is tender. Set aside.

Combine parsley, fontina cheese, and prosciutto in a small bowl; set aside.

Cook linguine in a Dutch oven according to package directions; drain. Return hot pasta to Dutch oven; immediately stir in egg yolks. Add bacon, onion, parsley mixture, heated cream, salt, pepper, and ½ cup Parmesan cheese.

Cook over low heat until thoroughly heated, stirring constantly. Transfer pasta to a serving dish; sprinkle with remaining ½ cup Parmesan cheese. Serve hot. **Yield: 8 servings.**

Saucy Manicotti

prep: 30 min.   cook: 10 min.   bake: 50 min.

Crusty cheese bubbling over gratin dishes and hiding a thick meat sauce will please anyone at your dinner table.

1	(8-ounce) package manicotti shells
1	(16-ounce) package Italian sausage, casings removed
1	large onion, chopped
9	garlic cloves, pressed
1	(26-ounce) jar seven-herb tomato pasta sauce
1	(8-ounce) container chive-and-onion cream cheese
6	cups (24 ounces) shredded mozzarella cheese, divided
¾	cup freshly grated Parmesan cheese
1	(15-ounce) container ricotta cheese
¾	teaspoon freshly ground pepper

Cook manicotti shells according to package directions, and drain.

Cook sausage, onion, and half of pressed garlic in a large Dutch oven over medium-high heat 6 minutes, stirring until sausage crumbles and is no longer pink. Stir in pasta sauce; bring to a boil. Remove from heat.

Preheat oven to 350°. Combine cream cheese, 4 cups mozzarella cheese, next 3 ingredients, and remaining pressed garlic in a large bowl, stirring until blended. Cut a slit down length of each cooked manicotti shell.

Spoon 1 cup sauce mixture into a lightly greased 13- x 9-inch baking dish. Spoon cheese mixture into manicotti shells, gently pressing cut sides together. Arrange stuffed shells over sauce in dish, seam sides down. Spoon remaining sauce over stuffed shells. Sprinkle with remaining 2 cups mozzarella cheese.

Bake, covered, at 350° for 50 minutes or until bubbly. **Yield: 7 servings.**

Note: For individual casseroles, spoon ¼ cup sauce into each of 7 lightly greased 8-ounce shallow baking dishes. Top each with 2 filled manicotti shells. Top with remaining sauce (about ¾ cup per dish) and remaining mozzarella cheese. Bake, uncovered, at 350° for 50 minutes.

Chicken Lasagna With Roasted Red Bell Pepper Sauce

prep: 20 min.   bake: 1 hr., 10 min.

A hot pan of lasagna tastes as good as anything in the world on a cold winter's night, especially when paired with a robust red wine.

4   cups finely chopped cooked chicken

2   (8-ounce) containers chive-and-onion cream cheese

1   (10-ounce) package frozen chopped spinach, thawed and well drained

1   teaspoon seasoned pepper

¾   teaspoon garlic salt

Roasted Red Bell Pepper Sauce

9   no-boil lasagna noodles

2   cups (8 ounces) shredded Italian three-cheese blend

Preheat oven to 350°. Stir together first 5 ingredients.

Layer a lightly greased 11- x 7-inch baking dish with one-third of Roasted Red Bell Pepper Sauce, 3 noodles, one-third of chicken mixture, and one-third of cheese. Repeat layers twice. Place baking dish on a baking sheet.

Bake, covered, at 350° for 50 to 55 minutes or until thoroughly heated. Uncover and bake 15 more minutes. **Yield: 6 to 8 servings.**

Roasted Red Bell Pepper Sauce

prep: 5 min.

This sauce is also great over your favorite noodles.

1   (12-ounce) jar roasted red bell peppers, drained

1   (16-ounce) jar creamy Alfredo sauce*

1   (3-ounce) package shredded Parmesan cheese

½   teaspoon dried crushed red pepper

Process all ingredients in a food processor until smooth, stopping to scrape down sides. **Yield: 3½ cups.**

*For testing purposes only, we used Bertolli Alfredo Sauce With Aged Parmesan Cheese.

Ultimate Nachos

prep: 13 min.   cook: 6 min.   bake: 8 min.

⅓   cup finely chopped onion

1   large garlic clove, minced

1   tablespoon olive oil

1   (16-ounce) can refried beans

½   cup fresh salsa

1   (13-ounce) package restaurant-style
     tortilla chips

1½ cups (6 ounces) shredded Monterey Jack
     cheese

1½ cups (6 ounces) shredded Cheddar cheese

Pickled jalapeño slices, well drained

1   cup guacamole (optional)

½   cup sour cream (optional)

Toppings: chopped fresh cilantro, sliced ripe olives,
     shredded lettuce, additional fresh salsa

Preheat oven to 450°. Sauté onion and garlic in hot oil in a skillet over medium heat 4 to 5 minutes or until onion is tender. Add beans and salsa to pan, stirring until beans are creamy. Cook 1 minute or until heated.

Scatter most of chips on a parchment paper-lined large baking sheet or an ovenproof platter. Top with bean mixture, cheeses, and desired amount of jalapeños.

Bake at 450° for 8 minutes or until cheese melts and edges are lightly browned.

Top with small dollops of guacamole and sour cream, if desired. Add desired toppings. Serve hot. **Yield: 6 to 8 appetizer servings.**

Taco Casserole

prep: 10 min.   cook: 10 min.   bake: 25 min.

Certainly tacos qualify as timeless comfort food. This dish makes use of all the familiar elements and then gets a nacho chip topping. Serve it with Lettuce Wedge Salad on page 115, and you've got a meal.

1	pound ground chuck
½	cup chopped onion
1	(1.25-ounce) package taco seasoning mix
1	(16-ounce) can chili beans, undrained*
1	(8-ounce) can tomato sauce
2	cups (8 ounces) shredded Colby cheese
5	cups coarsely crushed nacho cheese-flavored tortilla chips or other flavor tortilla chips (about 9 ounces)

Preheat oven to 350°. Brown ground chuck with onion in a large skillet over medium heat. Stir until beef crumbles and onion is tender; drain.

Return beef mixture to skillet; stir in taco seasoning, beans, and tomato sauce.

Layer half each of beef mixture, shredded cheese, and tortilla chips in a lightly greased 13- x 9-inch baking dish. Repeat procedure with remaining beef mixture, shredded cheese, and tortilla chips.

Bake, uncovered, at 350° for 25 minutes or until casserole is thoroughly heated. **Yield: 6 servings.**

*For testing purposes only, we used Bush's Best Chili Beans.

Homestyle Ground Beef Casserole

prep: 8 min.   cook: 15 min.   bake: 40 min.   stand: 15 min.

Hamburger casserole works for any weeknight and is a universal family favorite. Green beans and corn would round out the plate nicely.

1	pound ground round
1	(14½-ounce) can diced tomatoes with basil, garlic, and oregano, undrained
1	(10-ounce) can diced tomatoes and green chiles, undrained
1	(6-ounce) can tomato paste
1	teaspoon salt
½	teaspoon dried Italian seasoning
¼	teaspoon pepper
3	cups uncooked medium egg noodles
5	green onions, chopped
1	(8-ounce) container sour cream
1	(3-ounce) package cream cheese, softened
1	cup (4 ounces) shredded sharp Cheddar cheese
1	cup (4 ounces) shredded Parmesan cheese
1	cup (4 ounces) shredded mozzarella cheese

Cook ground round in a large skillet over medium heat 8 minutes, stirring until it crumbles and is no longer pink. Stir in both cans diced tomatoes and next 4 ingredients. Bring to a boil; reduce heat, and simmer, uncovered, 5 minutes. Remove from heat; set aside.

Preheat oven to 350°. Cook egg noodles in boiling salted water according to package directions; drain. Stir together hot cooked noodles, chopped green onions, sour cream, and cream cheese until blended.

Spoon egg noodles into a lightly greased 13- x 9-inch or other similar-size baking dish. Top with beef mixture; sprinkle with shredded cheeses in the order listed.

Bake, covered, at 350° for 35 minutes. Uncover and bake 5 more minutes. Let stand 10 to 15 minutes before serving. **Yield: 6 servings.**

Note: Freeze assembled, unbaked casserole up to 1 month, if desired. Thaw in refrigerator overnight. Bake as directed.

Twice-Baked Mashed Potatoes

prep: 15 min.   bake: 20 min.

A cross between twice-baked potatoes and really rich mashed potatoes, this casserole is a year-round winner. These potatoes are just as delicious if you substitute reduced-fat dairy products.

1	(22-ounce) package frozen mashed potatoes*
½	(8-ounce) package cream cheese, softened
½	cup sour cream
¼	cup chopped fresh chives
4	bacon slices, cooked and crumbled
½	teaspoon seasoned pepper
¼	teaspoon salt
½	cup (2 ounces) shredded Cheddar cheese

Garnish: fresh chives

Preheat oven to 350°. Prepare potatoes according to package directions.

Stir in cream cheese and next 5 ingredients. Spoon potatoes into a lightly greased 2-quart baking dish. Sprinkle with Cheddar cheese.

Bake at 350° for 20 minutes or until thoroughly heated. Garnish, if desired. **Yield: 6 servings.**

*For testing purposes only, we used Ore-Ida Frozen Mashed Potatoes. If you can't find frozen mashed potatoes, you can use 5½ cups leftover homemade mashed potatoes.

Sweet Potato Casserole

prep: 10 min.   bake: 30 min.

3½ cups mashed cooked sweet potatoes
½   cup butter, melted
¼   cup milk or half-and-half
2   large eggs
¾   cup sugar
1   teaspoon vanilla extract
3½ cups miniature marshmallows

Preheat oven to 375°. Process first 3 ingredients in a food processor until very smooth, about 2 minutes. Add eggs, sugar, and vanilla; process until blended. Pour into a greased 11- x 7-inch baking dish or other 2-quart baking dish.

Cover and bake at 375° for 10 minutes; uncover and sprinkle with marshmallows. Bake, uncovered, 15 to 20 minutes or until marshmallows are toasted. Serve hot. **Yield: 8 servings.**

Note: For best results, we recommend buying and cooking 3 large, deep orange sweet potatoes. Cut them in half crosswise; boil them in their skins 35 minutes or until very tender. Cool and slip potatoes out of their skins. Mash with a potato masher to equal 3½ cups. In a pinch, use 2 (29-ounce) cans candied yams as a substitute.

Mexican Rice-and-Cheese Casserole

prep: 12 min. bake: 30 min.

Here's a cheesy rice dish kids of any age will love. It pairs well with all things
Mexican, as well as with grilled chicken or shrimp. Chopped avocado makes
a fine accompaniment if you have time.

2   (8-ounce) packages Mexican Rice*
2   cups (8 ounces) shredded Monterey Jack
    cheese, divided
1   cup thinly sliced green onions
1   (8-ounce) container sour cream
1   teaspoon salt
¼   teaspoon ground red pepper
¼   teaspoon smoked or sweet paprika

Prepare rice according to package directions.
Preheat oven to 350°. Combine hot cooked rice,
1½ cups shredded cheese, and next 4 ingredients in a large bowl; stir until combined.
Transfer seasoned rice mixture to a greased
13- x 9-inch baking dish, and sprinkle with
remaining ½ cup cheese and paprika.
Bake, uncovered, at 350° for 25 to 30 minutes
or until thoroughly heated. **Yield: 10 servings.**

*For testing purposes only, we used Vigo
Mexican Rice.

Green Bean Casserole With Fried Leeks

prep: 10 min.   cook: 21 min.   bake: 5 min.

Remember the old green bean casserole made with convenience products: frozen or canned green beans, cream of mushroom soup, and French-fried onions? Here it is again, better than ever with some scrumptious flavor twists.

2   tablespoons butter
2   (8-ounce) packages sliced fresh mushrooms
1   teaspoon dried thyme
2   shallots, finely chopped
½   cup Madeira
1   cup whipping cream
1¼   pounds fresh green beans, trimmed
Vegetable or peanut oil
2   large leeks, cleaned and thinly sliced
       crosswise
Salt to taste

Melt butter in large heavy skillet over medium-high heat. Add mushrooms and thyme; sauté 5 minutes. Add shallots; sauté 3 minutes or until tender. Add Madeira, and cook over medium-high heat 3 minutes or until liquid evaporates. Add whipping cream, and cook 2 to 5 minutes or until slightly thickened. Remove from heat.

Meanwhile, cook beans in a small amount of boiling water 5 minutes or just until crisp-tender; drain. Add beans to mushroom mixture, and toss gently. Spoon into a greased 2-quart gratin dish or shallow baking dish. Cover and keep warm.

Preheat oven to 400°. Pour oil to a depth of 2 inches into a 3-quart saucepan; heat to 350°. Fry leeks, in 3 batches, 1 to 1½ minutes per batch or until golden. Remove leeks with a small metal strainer; drain on paper towels. Immediately sprinkle with salt. Sprinkle fried leeks over warm bean mixture.

Bake, uncovered, at 400° for 5 minutes or until casserole is thoroughly heated. **Yield: 6 servings.**

soups & stews

The Southern Art of Feeding

The fact that I love to feed people, especially men, used to give me a vague sense of discomfort. I mean, if I'm a modern, liberated woman, why do I derive such pleasure in the traditional task of making dinner? Why do I, like my grandmothers, circle the table like a glorified waitress, eager to refill iced tea glasses, to serve milk gravy, to lean over the men's shoulders and query them with yet another muffin? Isn't this blatantly unenlightened? Isn't a woman meant for more lofty endeavors than feeding?

That was before I gave birth to my first child and experienced the earthy, stark reality of being mammal—of breast-feeding a creature who grows, thrives, and survives solely on my instinctual need to feed. It was then I realized that offering sustenance to other human beings, i.e., preparing and serving food, is a powerful art that transcends all intellectual ideas of what women ought and ought not do. It's one thing I was born to do. Others may disagree, but for me, the need to feed is a legacy I now understand and fulfill without apology.

I suppose the art of feeding is universal, so it's with acknowledged bias that I suggest that Southerners do it with particular grace. Because of our rural heritage, we are free from the trappings of proper place settings, damask tablecloths, and fine china (except for special occasions), and we can concentrate instead on shucking 36 ears of corn. Volume counts—etiquette doesn't. When I was a child, my grandmother's table housed at least 10 different vegetable dishes and three kinds of pies. The assumption was that people were *hungry*. The point was to satisfy.

Last summer, a New York editor was visiting our home, and my sister-in-law, Haden, offered to come over and prepare a Southern meal for our guest and a group of friends.

continued

The story goes that she called her sister and told her about the event. She recited the menu she was preparing: fried chicken, black-eyed peas, fresh sliced tomatoes, fried corn, squash, okra, slaw, rice and gravy, cornbread, homemade biscuits, and black-bottom pie. Her sister exclaimed in all earnestness, "You mean you aren't baking a *ham!*"

I believe there's a kind of sensuality associated with the generosity of Southern feeding. We grow our vegetables. Our hands knead the earth. We've heard so many family stories of the men coming in hungry from the fields that we still respond accordingly, and that's all right by me.

Cooking is draped in a languid pace. You rise at dawn, and by the light of early morning you put the beans in the black pot and forget about them until dusk.

The other necessary ingredient to Southern feeding is that we serve it with grace. You may be tired and half-fried with anxiety yourself, but when friends come in, your face opens to smile as you take their hands and draw them into the heart of your kitchen. If it's an act—well, acting is an art, too.

We feed to nurture, to heal, to create, to enrich friendships, to gather family, to admit our inability to do anything else to comfort (as evidenced by day-of-the-funeral food we prepare and deliver). It's downright Biblical. I grew up Southern Baptist. Feeding the 5,000 was always a startling story to me, but I understood the concept. I guess by the time most of us Southerners are old, we've fed that many, too.

My daughter has a pet turtle. She will put lettuce in the terrarium and sit waiting, watching to see him eat what's been offered. Cedar waxwings collect berries just to share with their friends. Watch them sometimes beak-to-beak on a telephone wire. Perhaps, then, my need to feed really isn't a cultural imposition; it's a biological imperative. I still believe, though, it's imbued with a distinctly Southern style.

—Vicki Covington, Contributing Writer and Author of Numerous Books

Chicken-and-Wild Rice Soup

prep: 12 min.   cook: 6 hr.

This soup makes filling holiday fare and is a good use for leftover turkey (in place of chicken).

2	tablespoons butter
3	celery ribs, thinly sliced
1	medium onion, chopped
1	(8-ounce) package sliced fresh baby portobello mushrooms
2	teaspoons minced garlic
4	(14-ounce) cans seasoned chicken broth with roasted garlic*
3	cups chopped cooked chicken or turkey
1½	cups frozen whole kernel corn, thawed and drained
1	(8-ounce) can sliced water chestnuts, drained
1	cup uncooked wild rice
1	teaspoon salt
¾	teaspoon freshly ground pepper
2	cups whipping cream

Garnish: toasted slivered almonds

Melt butter in a large skillet over medium-high heat. Add celery and onion; cook 4 minutes or until almost tender. Add mushrooms and garlic; cook 2 minutes.

Combine mushroom mixture, broth, and next 6 ingredients in a 5-quart slow cooker.

Cover and cook on LOW 5 to 6 hours or until rice is tender. Stir in whipping cream. Garnish, if desired. **Yield: 12½ cups.**

*For testing purposes only, we used Swanson Seasoned Chicken Broth With Roasted Garlic.

Chicken Noodle Soup

prep: 25 min.   cook: 1 hr., 15 min.

Chicken soup still reigns as the ultimate food for the soul. This recipe is chock-full of good stuff. Use fresh vegetables if you prefer.

6   bone-in chicken breasts
1   celery rib with leaves
1¼ teaspoons salt
¼   teaspoon pepper
1   (16-ounce) package frozen mixed vegetables
1   small onion, chopped
¼   cup chopped fresh parsley or 1 tablespoon dried parsley flakes
2   (3-ounce) packages chicken-flavored ramen soup mix
Salt and pepper to taste

Bring 3 quarts water and first 4 ingredients to a boil in a large Dutch oven. Cover, reduce heat, and simmer 30 to 40 minutes or until chicken is tender. Remove chicken, reserving broth in Dutch oven. Skin, bone, and shred chicken.
Add mixed vegetables, onion, and parsley to reserved broth. Cover and cook over medium heat 20 minutes. Add ramen noodles with seasoning packet, and cook, stirring occasionally, 5 minutes. Stir in chicken, and cook 10 minutes. Season to taste with salt and pepper. **Yield: about 3 quarts.**

Beer-Cheese Soup

prep: 15 min.   cook: 16 min.

2½ cups milk
1   (12-ounce) bottle beer, divided
2   (5-ounce) jars process cheese spread*
1   (10½-ounce) can condensed chicken broth
½   teaspoon Worcestershire sauce
2   dashes hot sauce
3   tablespoons cornstarch

Combine milk and ¾ cup beer in a Dutch oven. Cook over medium heat, stirring constantly, 2 to 3 minutes or until thoroughly heated. **Add** cheese spread and next 3 ingredients. Cook over low heat, stirring constantly, until thoroughly heated.

Combine cornstarch and remaining beer; add to cheese mixture. Simmer, stirring constantly, 10 minutes or until thickened (do not boil). **Yield: 6 cups.**

*For testing purposes only, we used Kraft Sharp Old English Cheese in this recipe.

Note: If you prefer a soup with more of a bite, we suggest using a dark beer, such as Michelob Honey Lager.

Chicken Noodle Soup

"Baked" Potato Soup

prep: 21 min.   cook: 8 hr.

Who doesn't enjoy loading up a hot baked potato with the familiar three favorite toppings: sour cream, cheese, and bacon? In this recipe, all the goods are added to chunky soup.

6	large baking potatoes, peeled and cut into ½-inch cubes (about 3¾ pounds)
1	large onion, chopped (about 1½ cups)
3	(14-ounce) cans seasoned chicken broth with roasted garlic
¼	cup butter
2½	teaspoons salt
1¼	teaspoons freshly ground pepper
1	cup whipping cream or half-and-half
1	cup (4 ounces) sharp Cheddar cheese, shredded
3	tablespoons chopped fresh chives

Toppings: cooked and crumbled bacon, shredded Cheddar cheese, sour cream

Combine first 6 ingredients in a 5-quart slow cooker.

Cover and cook on HIGH 4 hours or on LOW 8 hours or until potatoes are tender.

Mash mixture until potatoes are coarsely chopped and soup is slightly thickened; stir in whipping cream, 1 cup cheese, and chives. Serve with desired toppings. **Yield: 12 cups.**

Caramelized Onion
Soup With Swiss Cheese-and-Basil Croutons

prep: 20 min.   cook: 46 min.   broil: 3 min.

French onion soup gets a flavor update with basil-flavored, crusty croutons.

6	medium onions, halved and thinly sliced
¼	cup olive oil
4	garlic cloves, pressed
3	tablespoons beef bouillon granules
1	teaspoon pepper
1	teaspoon chopped fresh thyme
2	tablespoons dry sherry (optional)
1	(8-ounce) French baguette
1	cup (4 ounces) finely shredded Swiss cheese
2	tablespoons chopped fresh basil
2	tablespoons mayonnaise

Cook sliced onions in hot oil in a Dutch oven over medium-high heat, stirring occasionally, 20 to 25 minutes or until onions are golden brown. Add garlic, and cook 1 minute. Stir in 8 cups water, bouillon granules, pepper, and thyme. Add sherry, if desired. Bring to a boil. Cover, reduce heat to low, and simmer, stirring occasionally, 20 minutes.

Ladle soup into oven-safe serving bowls, and place on a baking sheet.

Cut baguette diagonally into 8 slices. Stir together Swiss cheese, basil, and mayonnaise. Spread mixture on 1 side of bread slices. Top soup with bread slices, cheese side up.

Broil 5 inches from heat 2½ to 3 minutes or until lightly browned. Serve immediately.

Yield: 8 cups.

Black Bean Soup

prep: 20 min.   soak: 8 hr.   cook: 5 hr., 15 min.

Make this soup over the weekend, soaking the beans on Friday night and cooking them on Saturday. Serve with warmed flour tortillas or yellow rice.

1	(16-ounce) package dried black beans
3	chicken bouillon cubes
½	small onion
¼	small green bell pepper
6	garlic cloves, minced
2	tablespoons olive oil
1	teaspoon dried oregano
1	teaspoon ground cumin
1½	teaspoons sugar
1	teaspoon salt
½	teaspoon pepper

Garnish: minced red onion

Wash beans, and remove any foreign particles and debris.

Soak beans in water to cover in a 6-quart stockpot 8 hours. Rinse and drain beans.

Bring beans, 3 quarts water, and bouillon to a boil. Cover, reduce heat to low, and simmer 3 hours. Do not drain.

Process ½ small onion and bell pepper in a blender or food processor until smooth, stopping to scrape down sides.

Sauté garlic in hot oil in a large skillet over medium-high heat 1 minute. Add onion mixture, and cook, stirring constantly, 4 minutes.

Stir onion-and-garlic mixture into beans. Add oregano and next 4 ingredients. Simmer, uncovered, 1½ to 2 hours or until beans are tender and soup is thick. Garnish, if desired.

Yield: 8 servings.

Butternut Squash Soup

prep: 25 min.   cook: 50 min.

6   bacon slices
1   large onion, chopped
2   carrots, chopped
2   celery ribs, chopped
1   Granny Smith apple, peeled and finely chopped
2   garlic cloves, chopped
4   (12-ounce) packages frozen butternut squash, thawed
1   (32-ounce) container low-sodium, fat-free chicken broth
2   to 3 tablespoons fresh lime juice
1½ tablespoons honey
2   teaspoons salt
1   teaspoon ground black pepper
⅛   teaspoon ground allspice
⅛   teaspoon ground nutmeg
⅛   teaspoon ground red pepper
¼   cup whipping cream
Garnishes: sour cream, fresh thyme sprigs

Cook bacon slices in a Dutch oven until crisp. Remove bacon, and drain on paper towels, reserving 2 tablespoons drippings in Dutch oven. Coarsely crumble bacon, and set aside.

Sauté onion and carrots in hot bacon drippings in Dutch oven over medium-high heat 5 minutes or until onion is tender. Add celery and apple, and sauté 5 minutes. Add garlic, and sauté 30 seconds. Add butternut squash and chicken broth. Bring to a boil; reduce heat, and simmer 20 minutes or until carrots are tender.

Process squash mixture, in batches, in a blender or food processor until smooth.

Return to Dutch oven. Add lime juice and next 7 ingredients. Simmer 10 to 15 minutes or until thickened. Garnish, if desired. Top each serving with bacon. **Yield: 8 servings.**

30-Minute Chili

prep: 5 min.   cook: 25 min.

A homemade seasoning mix gives this quick chili great taste.

2   pounds lean ground beef
⅓   cup Chili Seasoning Mix
2   (14.5-ounce) cans diced tomatoes with
     green pepper, celery, and onion
2   (8-ounce) cans tomato sauce
1   (16-ounce) can black beans, undrained
1   (15.5-ounce) can small red beans, undrained
Toppings: corn chips, shredded Cheddar cheese

Cook beef in a Dutch oven over medium-high heat, stirring often, 4 to 5 minutes or until beef crumbles and is no longer pink; drain well. Return beef to Dutch oven; sprinkle with seasoning mix. Cook 1 minute over medium-high heat.

Stir in diced tomatoes and next 3 ingredients; bring to a boil over medium-high heat, stirring occasionally. Cover, reduce heat to low, and simmer, stirring occasionally, 15 minutes. Serve with desired toppings. **Yield: 8 servings.**

Chili Seasoning Mix

prep: 5 min.

This versatile mix yields big dividends in time-saving suppers. Loaded with flavor, it pairs perfectly with beef, pork, poultry, or seafood.

¾   cup chili powder
2   tablespoons ground cumin
2   tablespoons dried oregano
2   tablespoons dried minced onion
2   tablespoons seasoned salt
2   tablespoons sugar
2   teaspoons dried minced garlic

Stir together all ingredients. Store seasoning mix in an airtight container up to 4 months at room temperature. Shake or stir well before using. **Yield: about 1⅓ cups.**

Seafood Gumbo

prep: 1 hr., 5 min.   cook: 1 hr., 50 min.

This recipe serves a party crowd. It freezes well if you happen to have leftovers.

2	lemons, sliced
1	(3-ounce) package crab boil
1	teaspoon salt
2	pounds unpeeled medium-size raw shrimp
1	pound bacon
1	cup all-purpose flour
2	onions, finely chopped
2	green bell peppers, finely chopped
4	garlic cloves, minced
1	pound cooked ham, cubed
2	pounds fresh crabmeat, drained and flaked
3	pounds fresh okra, sliced
1	(28-ounce) can whole tomatoes, undrained and chopped
½	cup Worcestershire sauce
2	teaspoons salt
1	teaspoon pepper
	Hot cooked rice

Bring 1 gallon water, lemons, crab boil, and 1 teaspoon salt to a boil in a large Dutch oven. Add shrimp, and cook 3 to 5 minutes or until shrimp turn pink. Discard lemons and crab boil. Remove shrimp, reserving water. Peel shrimp. Chill.

Cook bacon in a large skillet until crisp; remove bacon, reserving drippings in skillet. Crumble bacon, and set aside.

Add flour to drippings in skillet; cook over medium heat, stirring constantly, until roux is caramel-colored (about 5 minutes). Stir in onions, bell peppers, and garlic; cook over low heat 10 minutes or until vegetables are tender.

Add roux, ham, and next 6 ingredients to reserved water in Dutch oven. Bring to a boil; reduce heat, and simmer 1 hour and 50 minutes. Stir in chilled shrimp, and cook 5 to 10 minutes. Serve gumbo over rice. Sprinkle with bacon. **Yield: 7½ quarts.**

Beef Daube

prep: 25 min.   cook: 3 hr., 28 min.   stand: 20 min.

Daube, a French country stew, is a homey dish made from simple ingredients. The secret to its rich flavor is to cook and cool it over a two-day period—a real bonus if you're looking for make-ahead menu options.

¼   cup olive oil or vegetable oil
1   (4-pound) boneless rump roast or chuck roast,
      well trimmed and cut into 1½- to 2-inch pieces
1½   teaspoons salt
1½   teaspoons freshly ground pepper
4   small yellow onions, cut into wedges
4   large carrots, scraped and cut into 2-inch
      pieces
1   garlic bulb, separated into cloves, each peeled
      and halved lengthwise
1   (14½-ounce) can Italian stewed tomatoes
1   (750-milliliter) bottle Cabernet Sauvignon;
      Côtes du Rhône; or other spicy, full-bodied
      red wine
Bouquet garni
Garnish: fresh thyme leaves

Heat oil in a Dutch oven over medium heat until hot. Sprinkle beef with salt and pepper. Cook beef in several batches in hot oil until browned on all sides. Remove beef to a large plate, reserving drippings in Dutch oven.
Sauté onions, carrots, and garlic in reserved drippings over medium heat 6 to 8 minutes. Add tomatoes and wine. Return beef to pan; add bouquet garni. Bring to a boil; cover, reduce heat, and simmer 1½ hours. Remove from heat, and cool completely. Cover pan, and refrigerate overnight.
Remove Dutch oven from refrigerator. Skim fat from surface, if desired. Let stew stand 20 minutes. Bring to a boil over medium heat; cover, reduce heat, and simmer 1 hour. Uncover and simmer 30 more minutes or until beef is very tender and stew is thickened. Discard bouquet garni before serving. Garnish, if desired.
Yield: 6 to 8 servings.

Note: A bouquet garni is a small bundle of fresh herbs, such as parsley, thyme, and bay leaves, tied together with kitchen twine. We tested with flat-leaf parsley, rosemary, thyme, and 2 bay leaves.

Easy Brunswick Stew

prep: 15 min.   cook: 50 min.

Make preparation a breeze by stopping at your local supermarket deli or favorite barbecue restaurant for shredded pork.

3	pounds shredded cooked pork
4	cups frozen cubed hash brown potatoes
3	(14½-ounce) cans diced tomatoes with garlic and onion
1	(14½-ounce) can whole kernel corn, drained
1	(14½-ounce) can cream-style corn
2	cups frozen lima beans
½	cup barbecue sauce
1	tablespoon hot sauce
1½	teaspoons salt
1	teaspoon pepper

Stir together shredded pork, 4 cups water, hash brown potatoes, and remaining ingredients in a 6-quart stockpot. Bring stew to a boil; cover, reduce heat, and simmer, stirring often, 45 minutes. **Yield: 5 quarts.**

My uncle Pat was a barbecue nut back before it became the suburban routine it is today. He had his own specially designed pit, just off his patio, and he cooked chicken and ribs every weekend. The barbecue was always great (basted only with lemon juice and butter), but the thing that made it special for me was a chicken-and-rice stew he would make to go along with it. It was especially good with a healthy dash of hot sauce.

—Clay Nordan, Managing Editor

desserts

Ice-Cream Sandwich Memories

When I was little, the threat of tornadoes in Alabama sent my mother's family into a tizzy. At my grandparents', it meant a scurry to the cellar, dug into the hillside behind the family farmhouse. I dreaded that, imagining spiders, scorpions, even snakes lurking among the store of potatoes, canning jars, and stakes for tomato plants.

When my family moved to Texas, twisters were a problem there, too. We had no basement or storm cellar, but when there was danger in the air, my mom made do. She'd drag the kitchen table, a '50s red top, into the hall and throw a mountain of pillows and quilts beneath the chrome legs. She'd shoo Toby the dog and me into that soft spot, grab books and a box of ice-cream sandwiches, and burrow in with us for the duration. Listening to her read, licking an ice-cream groove between the chocolate wafers, dodging Toby's greedy tongue—I felt utterly safe, and then some. Mom must have loved it, too, because sometimes just a rainy day was enough to build our shelter from the storm.

Now, many years gone by, and always at the thought of ice-cream sandwiches, comforting memories of that lovely little ritual stay with me, strong and sweet—just like my mom.

—Nancy Wyatt, Editor in Chief, Books

Old-Fashioned Peanut Butter Cookies

prep: 25 min.   chill: 3 hr.   bake: 8 min. per batch

These are big, chewy sugar-topped cookies for peanut butter fans of all ages.

1   cup butter, softened
1   cup creamy peanut butter
1   cup granulated sugar
1   cup firmly packed brown sugar
2   large eggs
2½ cups all-purpose flour
2   teaspoons baking soda
¼ teaspoon salt
1   tablespoon vanilla extract
Sugar

Beat butter and peanut butter at medium speed with an electric mixer until creamy; gradually add sugars, beating well. Add eggs, beating well.

Combine flour, soda, and salt in a medium bowl; gradually add to butter mixture, beating well after each addition. Stir in vanilla. Cover and chill dough 3 hours.

Preheat oven to 375°. Shape dough into 1½-inch balls; place 3 inches apart on ungreased baking sheets. Dip a fork in additional sugar; flatten cookies in a crisscross design.

Bake at 375° for 7 to 8 minutes. Remove to wire racks to cool. **Yield: 3 dozen.**

Note: For smaller cookies, shape dough into 1-inch balls, and bake 6 to 7 minutes. **Yield: 6 dozen.**

Cookies & Carburetors

My brother, Gary, never knew that my mom and I called them "tea parties." His guests at these afternoon soirees of hot, just-out-of-the-oven cookies and sweaty pitchers of iced tea were a bunch of teenage guy-friends. The party room was the most unconventional of places—our garage (aka "Harrington's auto shop"). Gary had the door flung open (DIY, not remote controlled); wrenches and shop-jacks were in motion; and talk of cams, valves, manifolds, and anything about cars was the chatter.

The caterer for their break time? Me—the younger sister. In our '60s kitchen with aqua-painted cabinets (still my favorite color), I baked cookies and served them to my "test subjects" at their get-togethers. Traditional cookies ruled: Favorites were peanut butter patterned by fork tines, crispy chocolate chip, snickerdoodles, and wedding cookies that just got better with each subsequent roll in powdered sugar. Gary's most requested were Spritz, or, as he to this day puts it, "the ones shot out of a can."

By the way, a timer wasn't needed to bake to perfection—I had Gary's lifelong buddy John Dutkin! Literally seconds before the timer was to go off, he'd fling open the kitchen door like a superhero and save us all from overcooked cookies. The Dutkin Principle now prevails in my kitchen: Never trust a buzzer. Your nose and instincts (with a measured dose of reality that cookies keep crisping after they're out of the oven) know best.

Recently, Gary Dale (let's call him by a proper Southern name) did me a favor, which I returned by fulfilling his request. "Send John cookies!" he declared. A hundred bucks later, and they were baked, shipped from Alabama to Florida, and on his doorstep. Dutkin, I hope you ate them in your garage, with a side of iced tea and memories that remind you that a little grime, good friends, and a batch of cookies will always go hand in hand.

—Shirley Harrington, Associate Food Editor

Chocolate Chip Cookies

prep: 10 min.   bake: 10 min. per batch

Extra stir-ins are what make a classic chocolate chip cookie unique. Here, chunks of milk chocolate candy bar and oats enhance the dough.

1   cup butter, softened
1   cup granulated sugar
1   cup firmly packed brown sugar
2   large eggs
2   teaspoons vanilla extract
2½ cups uncooked regular oats
2   cups all-purpose flour
1   teaspoon baking powder
½   teaspoon baking soda
½   teaspoon salt
1   (12-ounce) package semisweet chocolate
    morsels
3   (1.55-ounce) milk chocolate candy bars,
    coarsely chopped
1½ cups coarsely chopped pecans

Beat butter at medium speed with an electric mixer until creamy; add sugars, beating well. Add eggs and vanilla, beating until blended.

Process oats in a blender or food processor until finely ground. Combine oats, flour, and next 3 ingredients. Gradually add to butter mixture, beating well after each addition.

Stir in chocolate morsels, chopped candy bars, and pecans.

Preheat oven to 375°. Shape dough into 1½-inch balls, and place 2 inches apart on ungreased baking sheets.

Bake at 375° for 8 to 10 minutes or until lightly browned. Remove to wire racks to cool. **Yield: 7 dozen.**

Miss Lillian's Tea Cakes

When I was about 10, I spent many Saturdays at the family farm of my best friend, Sarah. On a glorious summer day, only one thing could coax us indoors: tea cakes fresh from the oven.

These heavenly treats would be baked for us by Sarah's grandmother, Miss Lillian. Though I'm well past my prime biking days, I'd gladly pedal 30 miles for just one more of her tea cakes.

A friend later shared a recipe that came close to them. For good measure, she threw in instructions for making homemade lemonade. The lemonade was a snap.

To be honest, I was nervous about making tea cakes, given that I'd never baked a cookie in my life. But the ingredient list was simple, and I had gotten a new mixer last Christmas, so making the dough was quite easy.

Of course, the real test is in the taste. The best tea cakes have the kind of sugared-butter goodness that will make you swear you just heard the *whap* of a screen door.

—Valerie Fraser Luesse,
Creative Development Director

Tea Cakes

prep: 20 min.   chill: 1 hr.
bake: 12 min. per batch   stand: 5 min.

This Southern favorite just says summertime. For the best results, chill the tea cake dough thoroughly before you roll and cut it.

1	cup butter, softened
2	cups sugar
3	large eggs
1	teaspoon vanilla extract
3½	cups all-purpose flour
1	teaspoon baking soda
½	teaspoon salt
Parchment paper	

Beat butter at medium speed with an electric mixer until creamy; gradually add sugar, beating well. Add eggs, 1 at a time, beating until blended after each addition. Add vanilla, beating until blended.

Combine flour, soda, and salt; gradually add flour mixture to butter mixture, beating at low speed until blended after each addition.

Divide dough in half; wrap each portion in plastic wrap, and chill 1 hour.

Preheat oven to 350°. Roll half of dough to ¼-inch thickness on a floured surface. Cut out cookies with a 2½-inch round cutter, and place 1 inch apart on parchment paper-lined baking sheets.

Bake at 350° for 10 to 12 minutes or until edges begin to brown; let stand on baking sheets 5 minutes. Remove to wire racks to cool. Repeat procedure with remaining dough.

Yield: 3 dozen.

Giant Oatmeal Cookies

prep: 19 min. bake: 18 min. per batch

A big, soft oatmeal cookie with raisins plus a cold glass of milk make the ideal afternoon snack at any age.

1	cup butter, softened
1	cup granulated sugar
1	cup firmly packed brown sugar
2	large eggs
1	tablespoon vanilla extract
2	cups all-purpose flour
1	teaspoon baking soda
½	teaspoon baking powder
½	teaspoon salt
1½	cups uncooked quick-cooking oats
1½	cups chopped pecans
1	cup raisins
Parchment paper	

Preheat oven to 350°. Beat butter at medium speed with an electric mixer until creamy; gradually add sugars, beating well. Add eggs and vanilla; beat well.

Combine flour and next 3 ingredients; gradually add to butter mixture, beating well after each addition. Stir in oats, pecans, and raisins.

Drop dough by ⅓ cupfuls 3 inches apart onto parchment paper-lined baking sheets.

Bake at 350° for 15 to 18 minutes or until just set and lightly browned. Cool slightly on baking sheets; remove to wire racks to cool completely. **Yield: 20 cookies.**

Note: To make 7 dozen regular-size oatmeal cookies, drop dough by heaping teaspoonfuls onto lightly greased baking sheets. Bake at 375° for 8 minutes or until lightly browned.

Double-Chocolate Brownies

prep: 15 min.   bake: 40 min.

Two kinds of chocolate lure you to try these rich brownies. No frosting needed.

2   (1-ounce) squares unsweetened chocolate
2   (1-ounce) squares semisweet chocolate
1   cup butter, softened
2   cups sugar
4   large eggs
1   cup all-purpose flour
½   teaspoon salt
2   teaspoons vanilla extract
¾   cup chopped toasted pecans
¾   cup semisweet chocolate morsels

Preheat oven to 350°. Microwave chocolate in a small microwave-safe bowl at MEDIUM (50% power) for 30-second intervals until melted (about 1½ minutes total time). Stir chocolate until smooth.

Beat butter and sugar at medium speed with an electric mixer until light and fluffy. Add eggs, 1 at a time, beating just until blended after each addition. Add melted chocolate, beating just until blended. Add flour and salt, beating at low speed just until blended.

Stir in vanilla, ½ cup pecans, and ½ cup chocolate morsels. Spread batter into a greased and floured 13- x 9-inch pan. Sprinkle with remaining ¼ cup pecans and ¼ cup chocolate morsels. **Bake** at 350° for 40 minutes or until set. Cool completely on a wire rack. Cut into squares. **Yield: 32 brownies.**

Note: Freeze brownies in an airtight container up to 1 month.

Lemon-Coconut Bars

prep: 10 min.   bake: 1 hr.

The recipe for Lemon Chess Pie Filling came to us from the Editor in Chief's late mother, Louise Floyd, of Potters Station, Alabama. It's a *Southern Living* favorite and the inspiration for this top-rated treat.

2   cups all-purpose flour
1   cup powdered sugar, divided
1   cup butter, softened
½   cup chopped slivered almonds, toasted
Lemon Chess Pie Filling
1   cup sweetened flaked coconut

Preheat oven to 350°. Combine flour and ½ cup powdered sugar. Cut butter into flour mixture with a pastry blender until crumbly; stir in almonds. Firmly press mixture into a lightly greased 13- x 9-inch pan.
Bake at 350° for 20 to 25 minutes or until light golden brown.
Stir together Lemon Chess Pie Filling and coconut; pour over baked crust.
Bake at 350° for 30 to 35 minutes or until set. Cool in pan on a wire rack. Sprinkle with remaining ½ cup powdered sugar, and cut into bars. **Yield: 32 bars.**

Lemon Chess Pie Filling

prep: 10 min.

2   cups sugar
4   large eggs
¼   cup butter, melted
¼   cup milk
1   tablespoon lemon zest
¼   cup fresh lemon juice
1   tablespoon all-purpose flour
1   tablespoon cornmeal
¼   teaspoon salt

Whisk together all ingredients. Use filling immediately. **Yield: about 3 cups.**

Pecan Pie Brownies

prep: 25 min.   bake: 50 min.

Two popular sweets—rich chocolate brownies and Southern pecan pie—unite in this unique dessert. And thanks to a jump start from frozen pie, it's ready for the oven with less than 30 minutes of hands-on prep time.

1	(2-pound) frozen pecan pie, thawed*
½	cup butter
1¾	cups (11.5-ounce package) semisweet chocolate chunks
1	cup sugar
2	large eggs
1	cup milk
1½	cups all-purpose flour
1	teaspoon baking powder

Cut pie into cubes. Set aside.

Microwave butter and chocolate chunks in a microwave-safe bowl at HIGH 1 minute. Stir and microwave 1 more minute. Stir until mixture is smooth.

Preheat oven to 350°. Beat chocolate mixture, sugar, eggs, milk, and half of pie cubes at low speed with a heavy-duty stand mixer until blended.

Add flour and baking powder, stirring with a wooden spoon until blended. Stir remaining half of pie cubes into batter. (Batter will be thick.) Spoon batter into a 13- x 9-inch pan coated with cooking spray.

Bake at 350° for 50 minutes. Cool brownies completely on a wire rack. Cut into squares.

Yield: 40 small or 20 large brownies.

*For testing purposes only, we used Edwards Frozen Pecan Pie. Take the frozen pie out of the freezer 2 hours before you need to prepare this recipe so that it has time to thaw.

Mississippi Mud

prep: 10 min.   bake: 32 min.

The origin of this luscious dessert can be found both as a pie and as a cake. Either way, it is Southern decadence at its best and is featured here as a gooey brownie hunk.

1½   cups all-purpose flour
2   cups sugar
½   cup unsweetened cocoa
2   teaspoons baking powder
½   teaspoon salt
1   cup butter, melted
4   large eggs, lightly beaten
1   tablespoon vanilla extract
1   cup chopped pecans
3   cups miniature marshmallows
Chocolate Frosting

Preheat oven to 350°. Combine first 5 ingredients in a large mixing bowl. Add butter, eggs, and vanilla, stirring until smooth. Stir in pecans. Pour batter into a greased and floured 13- x 9-inch pan.

Bake at 350° for 25 to 30 minutes or until a wooden pick inserted in center comes out clean. Immediately sprinkle marshmallows over top; return to oven, and bake 1 to 2 minutes. Remove from oven. Carefully spread Chocolate Frosting over marshmallows. Cool completely, and cut into squares. **Yield: 2 dozen.**

Note: For a hint of mocha, stir 1 tablespoon instant coffee powder into brownie batter along with dry ingredients.

Chocolate Frosting

prep: 5 min.

½   cup butter, melted
⅓   cup cocoa
⅓   cup evaporated milk
1   teaspoon vanilla extract
1   (16-ounce) package powdered sugar, sifted

Beat all ingredients at medium speed with an electric mixer until dry ingredients are moistened. Beat at high speed until frosting reaches spreading consistency. **Yield: 2½ cups.**

Mom's Apron Collection

Possibly inspired by Hollywood homemakers like June Cleaver and Harriet Nelson, or maybe by fancy electric home sewing machines, making aprons and swapping them was all the rage with my mom, her sisters, and my grandmother in the late '50s and early '60s. Mom's aprons had all the hallmarks of her new Singer. She'd take its fancy stitches out for a spin like a new sports car, zigzagging borders, racing through buttonholes, finishing with a flourish of decorative stitching.

I have a little collection of these aprons. There are chic, impractical cocktail aprons made of sheer organdy and elaborately trimmed, as well as sturdy little workhorses with roomy pockets made from recycled flour sacks, pieced like quilts and bordered with rickrack scraps. These everyday aprons' faded flower prints and subdued old stains tell of a splash of gravy here, a smear of frosting there, and frequent machine washing.

I've lost track of who made which apron, but I remember many a family gathering, the seven sisters plus sisters-in-law in those flirty little numbers, jostling for position in the crowded kitchen and vying for favorite dish.

—Nancy Wyatt, Editor in Chief, Books

Million-Dollar Pound Cake

prep: 20 min.   bake: 1 hr., 40 min.   cool: 1 hr., 15 min.

1   pound butter, softened
3   cups sugar
6   large eggs
4   cups all-purpose flour*
¾   cup milk
1   teaspoon almond extract
1   teaspoon vanilla extract
Garnishes: sweetened whipped cream,
      blueberries, sliced peaches

Preheat oven to 300°. Generously grease and lightly flour a 10-inch (14-cup) tube pan. (Use shortening to grease the pan, covering every nook and cranny. Sprinkle a light coating of flour over the greased surface. Tap out any excess flour.)

Beat butter at medium speed with an electric mixer until light yellow in color and creamy. (The butter will become a lighter yellow color; this is an important step, as the job of the mixer is to incorporate air into the butter so the cake will rise. It will take 1 to 7 minutes, depending on the power of your mixer.) Gradually add sugar, beating at medium speed until light and fluffy. Add eggs, 1 at a time, beating just until yellow disappears after each addition.

Add flour to butter mixture alternately with milk, beginning and ending with flour. Beat at low speed just until blended after each addition. (Batter should be smooth.) Stir in extracts. Pour batter into prepared pan.

Bake at 300° for 1 hour and 40 minutes or until a long wooden pick inserted in center comes out clean. Cool in pan on a wire rack 10 to 15 minutes. Remove from pan, and cool completely on wire rack. Garnish each serving, if desired. **Yield: 10 to 12 servings.**

*For testing purposes only, we used White Lily All-Purpose Flour.

A Passion for Pound Cake

I recently made a pound cake at home because my folks were coming from North Carolina for a visit. My mom always makes terrific pound cakes, and I felt panicky knowing that she, my dad, and sister were soon to be my jury.

Why was I so worried over one little recipe? So many of us stake our prowess in the kitchen on this golden favorite. Maybe a pound cake needs to be perfect because it's the hallmark of Southern hospitality. It's the handshake of friendship to a new neighbor or a tender beacon of sympathy for those who survive a loss. It's a happy catalyst of cozy chats and midnight snacks. Leftover slices often become breakfast for "the harried" or treats to put in the lunch box. Pound cakes nourish much more than the body. They feed the soul.

—Susan Dosier, Former Executive Editor

{ portable }

Banana Pound Cake

prep: 20 min.   bake: 1 hr., 20 min.
cool: 1 hr., 15 min.

This moist, full-flavored banana cake needs no ice cream or sauce to enhance its appeal. But if you insist, we recommend pralines-and-cream ice cream.

1½   cups butter, softened
3   cups sugar
5   large eggs
3   ripe bananas, mashed
3   tablespoons milk
2   teaspoons vanilla extract
3   cups all-purpose flour
1   teaspoon baking powder
½   teaspoon salt
¾   cup chopped pecans

Preheat oven to 350°. Beat butter at medium speed with an electric mixer about 2 minutes or until creamy. Gradually add sugar, beating 5 to 7 minutes. Add eggs, 1 at a time, beating just until yellow disappears after each addition. **Combine** mashed bananas, milk, and vanilla. **Combine** flour, baking powder, and salt; add to batter alternately with banana mixture, beginning and ending with flour mixture. Beat at low speed just until blended after each addition. Pour into a greased and floured 10-inch tube pan. Sprinkle with pecans. **Bake** at 350° for 1 hour and 20 minutes or until a long wooden pick inserted in center of cake comes out clean. Cool in pan on a wire rack 10 to 15 minutes; remove cake from pan, and let cool completely on wire rack. **Yield: 10 to 12 servings.**

Fresh Apple Upside-Down Cake

prep: 20 min.   cook: 7 min.   bake: 30 min.   cool: 5 min.

Tart apples that hold their shape when cooked, such as Granny Smith, are best for this recipe. A small paring knife makes quick work of peeling the fruit.

¾ cup butter, softened and divided
2   cups sugar, divided
3   large Granny Smith apples, peeled and cut into ½-inch-thick slices
1   cup chopped toasted pecans, divided
2   large eggs
1½ cups all-purpose flour
1   teaspoon baking powder
1   teaspoon ground cinnamon
½   cup milk

Melt ¼ cup butter in a 10-inch cast-iron skillet over medium-high heat; add 1 cup sugar, and cook, stirring often, 2 minutes or until sugar is melted and begins to turn golden. Add apple slices, and cook, stirring often, 5 minutes or until apples have softened slightly and juices are thickened and syrupy. Remove skillet from heat, and sprinkle apple mixture with ½ cup pecans. Set aside.

Preheat oven to 350°. Beat remaining ½ cup butter at medium speed with an electric mixer until creamy. Gradually add remaining 1 cup sugar, beating until light and fluffy. Add eggs, 1 at a time, beating just until blended after each addition.

Stir together flour, baking powder, and cinnamon; add to butter mixture alternately with milk, beating at low speed just until blended, beginning and ending with flour mixture. Stir in remaining ½ cup pecans. Spoon batter over apple mixture in skillet.

Bake at 350° for 30 minutes or until a wooden pick inserted in center comes out clean. Cool in skillet 5 minutes; invert onto a serving plate. **Yield: 8 servings.**

Gingerbread

prep: 15 min.   bake: 40 min.

Gingerbread is a truly old-fashioned treat. It's a homey dessert that celebrates fresh ground spices and is equally good served warm or at room temperature. Some prefer a whipped cream topping; others may enjoy it with Vanilla Sauce.

1	cup sugar
½	cup applesauce
¼	cup butter, softened or melted
¼	cup molasses
2	cups all-purpose flour
4	teaspoons ground ginger
1	teaspoon ground cinnamon
1	teaspoon baking soda
¼	teaspoon salt
1	cup fat-free buttermilk
2	large eggs, lightly beaten

Whipped cream (optional)
Vanilla Sauce (optional)

Preheat oven to 325°. Beat first 4 ingredients at medium speed with an electric mixer until blended.

Stir together flour and next 4 ingredients in a medium bowl. Combine buttermilk and eggs in a separate bowl. Add both mixtures alternately to butter mixture, beginning and ending with flour mixture. Beat at low speed until blended after each addition. Pour batter into a lightly greased 10-inch cast-iron skillet.

Bake at 325° for 35 to 40 minutes or until a wooden pick inserted in center comes out clean. If desired, serve with whipped cream or Vanilla Sauce. **Yield: 8 servings.**

Vanilla Sauce

prep: 5 min.   cook: 5 min.

2	tablespoons butter
1½	cups sugar
2	teaspoons all-purpose flour

Pinch of salt
| 2 | teaspoons vanilla extract |

Melt butter in a saucepan over medium heat. Add 1½ cups water.

Stir together sugar, flour, and salt. Gradually add sugar mixture to saucepan, stirring constantly. Bring to a boil, and cook, stirring constantly, until sauce is slightly thickened. Remove from heat; stir in vanilla. Cool completely. **Yield: 2 cups.**

Mama Dip's Carrot Cake

prep: 30 min.   bake: 52 min.   cool: 1 hr., 10 min.

This recipe from Chapel Hill, North Carolina, restaurateur Mildred "Mama Dip" Council makes one of the best carrot cakes we've tasted. The cake layers can be prepared ahead and frozen up to one month.

2   cups chopped walnuts
2½ cups self-rising flour
1½ teaspoons ground cinnamon
1   teaspoon baking soda
Parchment paper
2   cups sugar
1   cup vegetable oil
4   large eggs
3   cups grated carrots
5-Cup Cream Cheese Frosting (page 195)

Preheat oven to 350°. Arrange walnuts in a single layer in a shallow pan. Bake 12 minutes or until toasted and fragrant.

Sift together flour, cinnamon, and baking soda. Line bottoms of 3 lightly greased 9-inch round cake pans with parchment paper; lightly grease parchment paper.

Beat sugar and oil at medium speed with an electric mixer until smooth. Add eggs, 1 at a time, beating until blended after each addition. Gradually add flour mixture, beating at low speed just until blended after each addition. Fold in carrots and 1 cup toasted walnuts. Spoon batter into prepared pans.

Bake at 350° for 35 to 40 minutes or until a wooden pick inserted in center comes out clean. Cool in pans on wire racks 10 minutes; remove from pans to wire racks. Peel off parchment paper, and let cakes cool 1 hour or until completely cool.

Spread frosting between layers and on top and sides of cake; sprinkle remaining 1 cup toasted walnuts onto cake as desired. **Yield: 12 servings.**

Caramel Cake

prep: 15 min.   **bake: 35 min.**   **cool: 1 hr., 10 min.**

When caramel cake is on the menu, there's only one thing to say: It's all about the frosting!

1   (8-ounce) container sour cream
¼   cup milk
1   cup butter, softened
2   cups sugar
4   large eggs
2¾   cups all-purpose flour
2   teaspoons baking powder
½   teaspoon salt
1   teaspoon vanilla extract
Whipped Cream Caramel Frosting

Preheat oven to 350°. Combine sour cream and milk.

Beat butter at medium speed with an electric mixer until creamy. Gradually add sugar, beating well. Add eggs, 1 at a time, beating until blended after each addition.

Combine flour, baking powder, and salt; add to butter mixture alternately with sour cream mixture, beginning and ending with flour mixture. Beat at medium-low speed until blended after each addition. Stir in vanilla. Pour batter into 2 greased and floured 9-inch round cake pans.

Bake at 350° for 30 to 35 minutes or until a wooden pick inserted in center comes out clean. Cool in pans on wire racks 10 minutes. Remove from pans to wire racks, and let cool 1 hour or until completely cool.

Spread Whipped Cream Caramel Frosting between layers and on top and sides of cake. **Yield: 8 servings.**

Whipped Cream Caramel Frosting

prep: 7 min.   **cook: 6 min.**   **cool: 1 hr.**

1   cup unsalted butter
2   cups firmly packed dark brown sugar
¼   cup plus 2 tablespoons whipping cream
2   teaspoons vanilla extract
3¾   cups powdered sugar

Melt butter in a 3-quart saucepan over medium heat. Add brown sugar; bring to a boil, stirring constantly. Stir in whipping cream and vanilla; bring to a boil. Remove from heat, and let cool 1 hour. Transfer frosting to a mixing bowl.

Sift powdered sugar into frosting. Beat at high speed with an electric mixer until creamy and spreading consistency. **Yield: 3¾ cups.**

Red Velvet Layer Cake

prep: 15 min.   bake: 20 min.   cool: 1 hr., 10 min.

Classic red velvet cake holds memories for many people. Nowadays, there are red velvet cupcakes, cookies, cheesecakes, and sheet cakes, too. But at the end of the day, the three-layer cake stands tall and reigns supreme.

1   cup butter, softened
2½ cups sugar
6   large eggs
3   cups all-purpose flour
3   tablespoons unsweetened cocoa
¼   teaspoon baking soda
1   (8-ounce) container sour cream
2   teaspoons vanilla extract
2   (1-ounce) bottles red food coloring
5-Cup Cream Cheese Frosting

Preheat oven to 350°. Beat butter at medium speed with an electric mixer until creamy. Gradually add sugar, beating until light and fluffy. Add eggs, 1 at a time, beating just until blended after each addition.

Stir together flour, cocoa, and baking soda. Add to butter mixture alternately with sour cream, beginning and ending with flour mixture. Beat at low speed just until blended after each addition. Stir in vanilla; stir in red food coloring. Spoon cake batter into 3 greased and floured 8-inch round cake pans.

Bake at 350° for 18 to 20 minutes or until a wooden pick inserted in center comes out clean. Cool in pans on wire racks 10 minutes. Remove from pans to wire racks, and let cool 1 hour or until completely cool.

Spread 5-Cup Cream Cheese Frosting between layers and on top and sides of cake. **Yield: 12 servings.**

5-Cup Cream Cheese Frosting

prep: 10 min.

2   (8-ounce) packages cream cheese, softened
½   cup butter, softened
2   (16-ounce) packages powdered sugar
2   teaspoons vanilla extract

Beat cream cheese and butter at medium speed with an electric mixer until creamy. Gradually add powdered sugar, beating until fluffy. Stir in vanilla. **Yield: about 5 cups.**

White Chocolate-Raspberry Cheesecake

prep: 22 min.   bake: 58 min.   chill: 8 hr.

Raspberry preserves make a luscious layer within this cheesecake.

2   cups graham cracker crumbs
3   tablespoons sugar
½   cup butter, melted
5   (8-ounce) packages cream cheese, softened
1   cup sugar
2   large eggs
1   tablespoon vanilla extract
12   ounces white chocolate, melted and
      cooled slightly
¾   cup raspberry preserves
Garnish: fresh raspberries

Preheat oven to 350°. Combine first 3 ingredients; press crumb mixture into bottom of a lightly greased 9-inch springform pan. Bake at 350° for 8 minutes; cool slightly.

Beat cream cheese at medium speed with an electric mixer until creamy; gradually add 1 cup sugar, beating well. Add eggs, 1 at a time, beating after each addition. Stir in vanilla. Add melted white chocolate, beating well.

Microwave raspberry preserves in a small microwave-safe bowl at HIGH 30 seconds to 1 minute or until melted; stir well.

Spoon half of cream cheese batter into prepared crust; spread a little more than half of melted preserves over batter, leaving a ¾-inch border. Spoon remaining cream cheese batter around edges of pan, spreading toward the center. Cover remaining raspberry preserves, and chill.

Bake at 350° for 50 minutes or until cheesecake is just set and slightly browned. Remove from oven; cool completely on a wire rack. Cover and chill at least 8 hours.

Run a knife around edge of pan, and release sides. Reheat remaining preserves briefly in microwave to melt. Pour preserves over top of cheesecake, leaving a 1-inch border. Remove sides of pan. Garnish each serving, if desired. Store in refrigerator. **Yield: 12 servings.**

Note: To remove seeds from raspberry preserves, press preserves through a fine sieve using the back of a spoon, if desired.

German Chocolate Cheesecake

prep: 30 min.   bake: 45 min.   chill: 8 hr.   cook: 7 min.

With a nod to the classic three-layer cake, this luscious cheesecake takeoff comes pretty close to perfection.

1	cup chocolate wafer crumbs
2	tablespoons sugar
3	tablespoons butter, melted
3	(8-ounce) packages cream cheese, softened
¾	cup sugar
¼	cup unsweetened cocoa
2	teaspoons vanilla extract
3	large eggs
⅓	cup evaporated milk
⅓	cup sugar
¼	cup butter
1	large egg, lightly beaten
½	teaspoon vanilla extract
½	cup coarsely chopped pecans, toasted
½	cup organic coconut chips or flaked coconut

Preheat oven to 325°. Stir together first 3 ingredients; press into bottom of an ungreased 9-inch springform pan.

Bake at 325° for 10 minutes. Cool crust.

Increase oven temperature to 350°. Beat cream cheese and next 3 ingredients at medium speed with an electric mixer until blended. Add eggs, 1 at a time, beating just until blended after each addition. Pour into prepared crust.

Bake at 350° for 35 minutes. Remove from oven; run a knife around edge of pan. Cool completely in pan on a wire rack. Cover and chill 8 hours.

Stir together evaporated milk and next 4 ingredients in a saucepan. Cook over medium heat, stirring constantly, 7 minutes. Stir in pecans and coconut. Remove sides of pan; spread topping over cheesecake. **Yield: 12 servings.**

Warm Apple-Buttermilk Custard Pie

prep: 30 min.   bake: 1 hr., 10 min.   stand: 1 hr.

When fall rolls around and that first cool snap is in the air, celebrate with this comforting apple pie. Use your favorite pie-baking apple if you'd like.

½   (15-ounce) package refrigerated piecrusts
¼   cup butter
2   Granny Smith apples, peeled and sliced
¾   cup granulated sugar, divided
¾   teaspoon ground cinnamon, divided
¼   cup butter, softened
1⅓ cups granulated sugar
4   large eggs
2   tablespoons all-purpose flour
1   teaspoon vanilla extract
¾   cup buttermilk
3   tablespoons butter, softened
¼   cup firmly packed light brown sugar
½   cup all-purpose flour

Fit piecrust into a 9-inch pieplate according to package directions; fold edges under, and crimp. Prick bottom and sides of piecrust with a fork.

Melt ¼ cup butter in a large skillet over medium heat; add apples, ½ cup granulated sugar, and ½ teaspoon cinnamon. Cook, stirring occasionally, 3 to 5 minutes or until apples are tender; set aside.

Preheat oven to 300°. Beat ¼ cup butter and 1⅓ cups granulated sugar at medium speed with an electric mixer until creamy. Add eggs, 1 at a time, beating just until yellow disappears. Add 2 tablespoons flour and vanilla, beating until blended. Add buttermilk, beating until smooth.

Spoon apple mixture into piecrust; pour buttermilk mixture over apple mixture.

Bake at 300° for 30 minutes. Stir together 3 tablespoons butter, remaining ¼ cup granulated sugar, brown sugar, ½ cup flour, and remaining ¼ teaspoon cinnamon until crumbly. Sprinkle over pie. Bake 40 more minutes or until a knife inserted in center comes out clean. Let stand 1 hour before serving. **Yield: 8 servings.**

Classic Chess Pie

prep: 23 min. bake: 1 hr., 2 min.

½ (15-ounce) package refrigerated piecrusts
2   cups sugar
2   tablespoons cornmeal
1   tablespoon all-purpose flour
¼   teaspoon salt
½   cup butter, melted
¼   cup milk
1   tablespoon white vinegar
½   teaspoon vanilla extract
4   large eggs, lightly beaten

Preheat oven to 425°. Fit piecrust into a 9-inch pieplate according to package directions; fold edges under, and crimp.

Line piecrust with aluminum foil, and fill with pie weights or dried beans.

Bake at 425° for 4 to 5 minutes. Remove weights and foil; bake 2 more minutes or until golden. Cool completely.

Reduce oven temperature to 350°. Stir together sugar and next 7 ingredients until blended. Add eggs, stirring well. Pour filling into pre-baked crust.

Bake at 350° for 50 to 55 minutes, shielding edges with aluminum foil after 10 minutes to prevent excessive browning. Cool completely on a wire rack. **Yield: 8 servings.**

Banana Pudding Pie

prep: 20 min.   bake: 24 min.   cool: 1 hr., 30 min.   chill: 4 hr.

Pie just doesn't get any better than this tasty twist on banana pudding. Hang onto your egg yolks—you'll be using them in the Vanilla Cream Filling.

1   (12-ounce) box vanilla wafers, divided
½   cup butter, melted
2   large bananas, sliced
Vanilla Cream Filling
4   egg whites
½   cup sugar

Preheat oven to 350°. Set aside 30 vanilla wafers; pulse remaining vanilla wafers in a food processor 8 to 10 times or until coarsely crushed. (Yield should be about 2½ cups.) Stir together crushed vanilla wafers and butter until blended. Firmly press on bottom, up sides, and onto lip of a 9-inch pieplate.

Bake at 350° for 10 to 12 minutes or until lightly browned. Remove to a wire rack, and let cool 30 minutes or until completely cool.

Arrange banana slices over bottom of crust. Prepare Vanilla Cream Filling, and spread half of hot filling over bananas; top with 20 vanilla wafers. Spread remaining hot filling over vanilla wafers. (Filling will be about ¼ inch higher than top edge of crust.)

Beat egg whites at high speed with an electric mixer until foamy. Add sugar, 1 tablespoon at a time, beating until stiff peaks form and sugar dissolves. Spread meringue over hot filling, sealing edges.

Bake at 350° for 10 to 12 minutes or until golden brown. Remove from oven, and let cool 1 hour on a wire rack or until completely cool. Coarsely crush remaining 10 vanilla wafers, and sprinkle over top of pie. Chill 4 hours. Store leftovers in refrigerator. **Yield: 8 servings.**

Vanilla Cream Filling

prep: 5 min.   cook: 10 min.

¾   cup sugar
⅓   cup all-purpose flour
2   large eggs
4   egg yolks
2   cups milk
2   teaspoons vanilla extract

Whisk together first 5 ingredients in a heavy saucepan. Cook over medium-low heat, whisking constantly, 8 to 10 minutes or until mixture reaches the thickness of chilled pudding. (Mixture will just begin to bubble and will be thick enough to hold soft peaks when whisk is lifted.) Remove from heat, and stir in vanilla. Use immediately. **Yield: 2½ cups.**

Coconut Cream Pie

prep: 20 min.   bake: 12 min.   cook: 11 min.   stand: 5 min.   chill: 4 hr.

In true diner style, this coconut pie has a thick, buttery filling and a mountain of whipped cream on top.

½   (15-ounce) package refrigerated piecrusts
½   cup sugar
¼   cup cornstarch
2   cups half-and-half
4   egg yolks
3   tablespoons butter
1   cup sweetened flaked coconut
2½   teaspoons vanilla extract, divided
2   cups whipping cream
⅓   cup sugar
Garnish: toasted coconut

Preheat oven to 450°. Fit piecrust into a 9-inch pieplate according to package directions; fold edges under, and crimp. Prick bottom and sides of piecrust with a fork.

Bake at 450° for 10 to 12 minutes or until lightly browned. Cool crust on a wire rack.

Combine ½ cup sugar and cornstarch in a heavy saucepan. Whisk together half-and-half and egg yolks. Gradually whisk egg mixture into sugar mixture; bring to a simmer over medium heat, whisking constantly. Simmer, whisking constantly, 3 minutes; remove from heat. Stir in butter until it melts; stir in 1 cup coconut and 1 teaspoon vanilla.

Place saucepan in an ice-water bath for 5 minutes or until filling is slightly warm, gently stirring occasionally. Pour filling into prepared crust. Place plastic wrap directly on custard (to prevent a film from forming). Place pie in refrigerator for 4 hours or until thoroughly chilled.

Beat whipping cream at high speed with an electric mixer until foamy; gradually add ⅓ cup sugar and remaining 1½ teaspoons vanilla, beating until soft peaks form. Spread whipped cream over filling. Garnish, if desired. **Yield: 8 servings.**

Note: For dramatic effect, we garnished the pie with organic coconut chips. Find them at organic food stores. You could also use sweetened flaked coconut.

Lemon Meringue Pie

prep: 25 min. bake: 32 min.

Get ready for some down-home comfort with this tangy-tart lemon pie featuring a flaky crust. To cut clean slices, dip your knife blade into cold water between cuts.

½ (15-ounce) package refrigerated piecrusts
Lemon Meringue Pie Filling
6 egg whites
½ teaspoon vanilla extract
6 tablespoons sugar

Preheat oven to 450°. Fit piecrust into a 9-inch pieplate according to package directions; fold edges under, and crimp. Prick bottom and sides of piecrust with a fork.
Bake at 450° for 10 to 12 minutes or until lightly browned. Cool crust on a wire rack. Reduce oven temperature to 325°.

Prepare Lemon Meringue Pie filling; remove from heat, and cover pan. (Proceed immediately to next step to ensure that meringue is spread over pie while filling is *hot*.)
Beat egg whites and vanilla at high speed with an electric mixer until foamy. Add sugar, 1 tablespoon at a time, and beat until stiff peaks form. Pour hot filling into prepared crust. Spread meringue over filling, sealing edges.
Bake at 325° for 20 minutes or until golden. Cool pie completely on a wire rack. Store pie in refrigerator. **Yield: 6 to 8 servings.**

Lemon Meringue Pie Filling

prep: 10 min. cook: 10 min.

1 cup sugar
¼ cup cornstarch
⅛ teaspoon salt
4 large egg yolks
2 cups milk
⅓ cup fresh lemon juice
3 tablespoons butter
1 teaspoon lemon zest
½ teaspoon vanilla extract

Whisk together first 3 ingredients in a medium-size heavy saucepan. Whisk in egg yolks, milk, and lemon juice. Bring to a boil over medium heat, whisking constantly. Cook, whisking constantly, 2 minutes; remove pan from heat. Stir in butter until it melts; stir in lemon zest and vanilla. **Yield: enough for 1 (9-inch) pie.**

Note: It's easier to remove the zest from lemons before juicing them.

Peanut Butter Pie

prep: 15 min.   bake: 8 min.   cook: 15 min.   chill: 3 hr.

This pie filling is as rich as they come, and it's enhanced by a peanutty graham cracker crust.

1¼ cups graham cracker crumbs
⅓ cup dry-roasted peanuts, coarsely ground
2 tablespoons granulated sugar
¼ cup plus 2 tablespoons butter, melted
⅔ cup granulated sugar
3 tablespoons cornstarch
¼ teaspoon salt
2½ cups evaporated milk
2 egg yolks, lightly beaten
½ cup peanut butter
½ cup peanut butter morsels
1 teaspoon vanilla extract
½ cup whipping cream
1 tablespoon powdered sugar
¼ teaspoon vanilla extract
Chopped dry-roasted peanuts

Preheat oven to 350°. Combine first 3 ingredients; stir in melted butter. Firmly press crumb mixture into a lightly greased 9-inch pieplate. **Bake** at 350° for 8 minutes or until browned. Set aside to cool.

Combine ⅔ cup sugar, cornstarch, and salt in a heavy saucepan. Gradually stir in evaporated milk. Cook over medium heat, stirring constantly, until mixture is thickened and bubbly. Gradually stir about one-fourth of hot mixture into beaten egg yolks; add to remaining hot mixture, stirring constantly. Cook, stirring constantly with a wire whisk, 3 minutes or until thickened. Remove from heat. Stir in peanut butter, morsels, and 1 teaspoon vanilla. Stir until morsels melt.

Pour filling into prebaked crust. Cover and chill pie 3 hours or until firm.

Beat whipping cream at medium speed with an electric mixer until foamy; add powdered sugar and ¼ teaspoon vanilla, and beat until soft peaks form. Top each serving with whipped cream, and sprinkle with chopped peanuts.
Yield: 8 servings.

Classic Strawberry Shortcake

prep: 20 min.   stand: 2 hr.   bake: 15 min.

This summertime favorite shows off juicy strawberries like no other dessert, though sliced peaches are equally nice as an option. If your berries are really sweet, decrease the sugar to suit your taste. Drop the dough easily by using a lightly greased ⅓-cup dry measure.

2	(16-ounce) containers fresh strawberries, sliced or quartered
¾	cup sugar, divided
¼	teaspoon almond extract (optional)
1	cup whipping cream
2	tablespoons sugar
2¾	cups all-purpose flour
4	teaspoons baking powder
¾	cup cold butter, cut up
2	large eggs, lightly beaten
1	(8-ounce) container sour cream
1	teaspoon vanilla extract

Garnish: fresh strawberries with leaves

Combine strawberries, ½ cup sugar, and, if desired, almond extract. Cover berry mixture, and let stand 2 hours.

Beat whipping cream at medium speed with an electric mixer until foamy; gradually add 2 tablespoons sugar, beating until soft peaks form. Cover and chill up to 2 hours.

Preheat oven to 450°. Combine flour, remaining ¼ cup sugar, and baking powder in a large bowl; cut butter into flour mixture with a pastry blender or 2 forks until crumbly.

Whisk together eggs, sour cream, and vanilla until blended; add to flour mixture, stirring just until dry ingredients are moistened. Drop dough by lightly greased ⅓ cupfuls onto a lightly greased baking sheet. (Coat cup with vegetable cooking spray after each drop.)

Bake at 450° for 12 to 15 minutes or until golden.

Split shortcakes in half horizontally. Spoon about ½ cup berry mixture onto each shortcake bottom; top each with a rounded tablespoon of chilled whipped cream and a shortcake top. Serve with remaining whipped cream. Garnish, if desired. **Yield: 8 servings.**

Country Peach Cobbler

prep: 35 min.   stand: 10 min.   bake: 42 min.

This cobbler not only has its share of fresh peaches, but also two crisp layers of pastry. If your peaches are really juicy, slide a foil-lined baking sheet underneath the baking dish in the oven to catch any drips.

12   medium to large fresh peaches, peeled and
      sliced (about 12 cups)
3   cups sugar
⅓   cup all-purpose flour
⅔   cup butter
1   tablespoon vanilla extract
2   (15-ounce) packages refrigerated piecrusts
2   tablespoons sugar
Vanilla ice cream

Combine first 3 ingredients in a Dutch oven, and let stand 10 minutes or until sugar dissolves. Bring peach mixture to a boil; reduce heat to low, and simmer 10 minutes or until tender. Remove pan from heat; add butter and vanilla, stirring until butter melts.

Preheat oven to 475°. Unroll piecrusts. Cut 1½ crusts into 1½-inch-wide strips for the lattice top. Place strips in refrigerator. Trim another 1½ crusts to fit a 13- x 9-inch baking dish.

Spoon half of peach mixture into a lightly greased 13- x 9-inch baking dish. Arrange trimmed crusts over peach filling, overlapping slightly, if necessary. Cut several slits in pastry. **Bake** at 475° for 20 to 22 minutes or until pastry is well browned. Remove from oven; cool slightly. Spoon remaining peach mixture over baked pastry. Carefully arrange pastry strips in a lattice design over hot filling. Sprinkle with 2 tablespoons sugar. Bake 20 more minutes or until top pastry is well browned. Serve warm or cold with vanilla ice cream. **Yield: 8 to 10 servings.**

Note: If peaches aren't in season, you can substitute 2 (20-ounce) packages frozen peaches. Reduce sugar to 2 cups and flour to 3 tablespoons. Proceed as directed. **Yield: 8 to 10 servings.**

Berry Pickin'

Growing up, I spent many summer afternoons at my grandmother's farm picking the abundant blackberries that grew wild in the pasture around her home. What stands out in my mind is Grannie's unusual method for picking blackberries. My brother, sister, and I would climb into the bucket on the front of her tractor, and she would drive us down to the pasture where the bushes were. Once there, she would lower the bucket right into the middle of the bushes; we would sit and pick berries from that perch. Occasionally, she would climb over the top of the tractor to join us.

With purple-stained hands and tongues, we would ride back to the barn to put away the tractor and then follow Grannie inside to watch her wash the berries and make cobbler. The lattice top was made of biscuit dough sprinkled with sugar. As soon as the cobbler came out of the oven, I would tear off pieces of crust and dip them in the blackberry juice. Thinking about it makes my mouth water! However, my grandmother didn't like serving cobbler that was missing most of its crust, so she began making me a separate dish with extra crust for dipping.

—Paula Hughes, Copy Chief

Blackberry Cobbler

prep: 12 min.   bake: 30 min.

1	cup sugar
¼	cup all-purpose flour
5	cups fresh blackberries or 2 (14-ounce) packages frozen blackberries, thawed and drained
1	tablespoon lemon juice
Crust	
2	tablespoons butter, melted
1	teaspoon sugar

Preheat oven to 425°. Combine 1 cup sugar and flour; add berries, and toss well. (If using frozen berries, increase flour to ⅓ cup.) Sprinkle with lemon juice. Spoon into a greased 8- or 9-inch square baking dish.
Prepare Crust, and spoon 9 mounds over blackberries. Brush with butter, and sprinkle with 1 teaspoon sugar.
Bake, uncovered, at 425° for 30 minutes or until browned and bubbly. Serve warm with ice cream, if desired. **Yield: 9 servings.**

Crust

prep: 10 min.

1¾	cups all-purpose flour
3	tablespoons sugar
1½	teaspoons baking powder
¾	teaspoon salt
¼	cup shortening
½	cup whipping cream
½	cup buttermilk

Combine first 4 ingredients; cut in shortening with a pastry blender until mixture is crumbly. Stir in whipping cream and buttermilk just until blended. **Yield: enough topping for 1 cobbler.**

Bananas Foster Gratin

prep: 10 min.   cook: 4 min.   bake: 10 min.

Get all the flavor without the flame in this version of the famous dessert.

¼   cup firmly packed light brown sugar
1   tablespoon dark rum
¼   teaspoon ground cinnamon
2   teaspoons butter
4   medium-size ripe bananas
1   almond biscotti, crushed (about ⅓ cup)
Vanilla ice cream

Preheat oven to 450°. Stir together first 3 ingredients and 3 tablespoons water in a 10-inch skillet over medium heat; bring to a boil. Reduce heat to medium-low, and simmer, stirring constantly, 2 minutes. Remove from heat, and stir in butter.

Slice bananas diagonally. Add to brown sugar mixture in skillet, tossing to coat.

Spoon banana mixture into 4 lightly greased (1- to 1½-cup) gratin dishes or a shallow, lightly greased 1-quart baking dish.

Bake at 450° for 10 minutes or until bubbly. Remove from oven, and sprinkle with biscotti crumbs. Serve warm with vanilla ice cream.

Yield: 4 servings.

Apple Brown Betty

prep: 15 min. bake: 55 min.

4   cups soft white breadcrumbs
⅓   cup butter, melted
1   cup firmly packed brown sugar
1   tablespoon ground cinnamon
4   large apples, peeled and cut into
      ¼-inch-thick slices
1   cup apple cider

Preheat oven to 350°. Stir together bread-crumbs and butter.

Stir together brown sugar and cinnamon. Place half of the apple slices in a lightly greased 8-inch square baking dish; sprinkle apples with half of brown sugar mixture and half of breadcrumb mixture. Repeat procedure with remaining apples, brown sugar mixture, and breadcrumb mixture. Pour apple cider over top. **Bake** at 350° for 45 to 55 minutes or until browned. **Yield: 6 servings.**

Sautéed Brown Sugar Pears

prep: 15 min. cook: 7 min.

A simple skillet pear dish gets dressed up with crème fraîche and gingersnap crumbs. This recipe can be doubled easily.

1   tablespoon lemon juice
3   Anjou pears, peeled and quartered
3   tablespoons butter
¼   cup firmly packed brown sugar
1   teaspoon vanilla extract
Crème fraîche or vanilla ice cream
Gingersnaps, crumbled

Sprinkle lemon juice over pears; toss. Melt 1 tablespoon butter in a large nonstick skillet over medium-high heat. Sauté pears 2 minutes or until browned. Add remaining 2 tablespoons butter and brown sugar to skillet. Reduce heat to medium-low; cook, stirring often, 3 to 4 minutes or until pears are tender. Remove from heat, and stir in vanilla extract. Serve warm pears and syrup with a dollop of crème fraîche or ice cream. Sprinkle with gingersnap crumbs. **Yield: 4 servings.**

Bread Pudding With Rum Sauce

prep: 15 min.   bake: 50 min.

Day-old bread is best for soaking up the liquid in this comforting dessert. The easy Rum Sauce makes each serving luscious.

4	large eggs
1½	cups sugar
3	(12-ounce) cans evaporated milk
½	cup butter, melted
1	tablespoon vanilla extract
2	teaspoons ground cinnamon
6	cups torn, packed French bread
1	large Granny Smith apple, peeled and chopped
1½	cups coarsely chopped walnuts, toasted
1	cup golden raisins

Rum Sauce

Preheat oven to 350°. Whisk eggs in a large bowl. Whisk in sugar and next 4 ingredients. Fold in bread and next 3 ingredients, stirring until bread is moistened. Pour into a greased 13- x 9-inch baking dish.

Bake, uncovered, at 350° for 50 minutes or until set. Cut into squares. Serve warm with Rum Sauce. **Yield: 12 servings.**

Rum Sauce

prep: 2 min.   cook: 3 min.

2	(14-ounce) cans sweetened condensed milk
2	tablespoons dark rum
1	tablespoon vanilla extract

Pour condensed milk into a small saucepan; cook over medium heat until hot, stirring often. Remove from heat, and stir in rum and vanilla. Serve warm. **Yield: 2½ cups.**

Creamy Rice Pudding With Praline Sauce

prep: 15 min.   cook: 50 min.

If you're a fan of pure and simple old-fashioned desserts, this dish is for you. The praline sauce takes it to the next level.

2   cups milk
1   cup uncooked extra long-grain white rice*
½   teaspoon salt
2¾ cups half-and-half, divided
4   egg yolks, beaten
½   cup sugar
1½ teaspoons vanilla extract
20 caramels
½   cup chopped toasted pecans

Stir together first 3 ingredients and 2 cups half-and-half in a large saucepan. Cover and cook over medium-low heat, stirring often, 35 to 40 minutes or until rice is tender.

Whisk together egg yolks, ½ cup half-and-half, and sugar. Gradually stir about one-fourth of hot rice mixture into yolk mixture; stir yolk mixture into remaining hot mixture. Cook over medium-low heat, stirring constantly, until mixture reaches 160° and is thickened and bubbly (about 7 minutes). Remove from heat; stir in vanilla.

Stir together caramels and remaining ¼ cup half-and-half in a small saucepan over medium-low heat until smooth. Stir in pecans. Serve praline sauce over rice pudding. **Yield: 6 to 8 servings.**

*For testing purposes only, we used Mahatma Rice.

Chocolate Pudding

prep: 15 min.   cook: 16 min.

Here's a really rich but simple homemade pudding. A small serving will satisfy.

⅓   cup cornstarch
4   cups whipping cream
1   cup sugar
1   cup semisweet chocolate morsels
1   tablespoon vanilla extract
⅛   teaspoon salt

Combine cornstarch and ½ cup water, stirring until smooth. Bring whipping cream to a simmer in a 2-quart saucepan over medium heat. Stir in cornstarch mixture, sugar, and remaining ingredients, stirring constantly until chocolate melts. Cook pudding, stirring constantly, 8 minutes or until thick and creamy. Serve warm or chilled. **Yield: 5 cups.**

Pound Cake Banana Pudding

prep: 20 min.   cook: 15 min.   chill: 6 hr.   bake: 15 min.

This recipe was inspired by the pudding served at the famous Mrs. Wilkes' Dining Room in Savannah, Georgia—a family-style comfort-food restaurant to write home about.

4   cups half-and-half
4   egg yolks
1½ cups sugar
¼   cup cornstarch
¼   teaspoon salt
3   tablespoons butter
2   teaspoons vanilla extract
1   (1-pound) pound cake, cubed*
4   large ripe bananas, sliced
Meringue

Whisk together first 5 ingredients in a saucepan over medium-low heat; cook, whisking constantly, 13 to 15 minutes or until thickened. Remove from heat; add butter and vanilla, stirring until butter melts.

Layer half of pound cake cubes, half of bananas, and half of pudding mixture in a lightly greased 3-quart round baking dish. Repeat layers. Cover pudding, and chill 6 hours.

Preheat oven to 375°. Prepare Meringue, and spread over pudding.

Bake at 375° for 15 minutes or until golden brown. Spoon into glasses, if desired. **Yield: 10 to 12 servings.**

*For testing purposes only, we used Sara Lee Family Size All Butter Pound Cake.

Meringue

prep: 10 min.

¼   cup sugar
⅛   teaspoon salt
4   egg whites
¼   teaspoon vanilla extract

Combine sugar and salt.

Beat egg whites and vanilla at high speed with an electric mixer until foamy. Add sugar mixture, 1 tablespoon at a time, and beat 2 to 3 minutes or until stiff peaks form and sugar dissolves. **Yield: about 3½ cups.**

Mocha Pudding Cake

prep: 15 min.   bake: 30 min.

We're nearly certain that just pondering the concept of this gooey chocolate cake with a thick pudding underneath will make you want to eat dessert first.

1   cup all-purpose flour
1½   teaspoons baking powder
¼   teaspoon salt
1   cup sugar, divided
6   tablespoons unsweetened cocoa, divided
½   cup milk
3   tablespoons canola oil
1   teaspoon vanilla extract
½   cup semisweet chocolate mini morsels
1   cup strong brewed coffee
Vanilla ice cream (optional)

Preheat oven to 350°. Combine first 3 ingredients, ⅔ cup sugar, and 4 tablespoons cocoa in a large bowl. Stir together milk, canola oil, and vanilla; add to dry ingredients, stirring just until blended. Spread batter into a lightly greased 8-inch square pan.

Combine chocolate morsels, remaining ⅓ cup sugar, and remaining 2 tablespoons cocoa. Sprinkle over batter.

Bring coffee to a boil; pour boiling coffee over batter. (Do not stir.)

Bake at 350° for 25 to 30 minutes or until cake springs back when lightly pressed in center. Serve warm with ice cream, if desired. **Yield: 6 to 8 servings.**

Just a Little Flavoring

Boiled custard is one of those old-fashioned dessert drinks you hardly ever hear of anymore. But for me, it simply wouldn't be Christmas without my mother's homemade recipe and the tradition that goes along with it.

My family still operates a dairy farm in Tennessee, where fresh milk flows abundantly. On Christmas Eve, my mother sets a gallon jug by the back door, a not-so-subtle hint that anyone going to the barn should take it and return it filled with milk.

When the courier, usually one of my brothers, completes the errand, he simply puts the jar inside the door, knocks loudly, and shouts, "Mama, here's your milk." She then transports the creamy goodness straight to a pot on the stovetop and begins the transformation.

Some people like their boiled custard thick enough to eat with a spoon, but we prefer the dish velvety smooth and drinkable. My grandmother served hers over a scoop of vanilla ice cream. My sister likes it with a dollop of homemade whipped cream. The rest of us add a drop or two of "flavoring" to jazz up the glass.

You see, we were never allowed to drink liquor at my mother's house. Still aren't, for that matter. But she grudgingly turns a blind eye to the brown paper bag that appears around the dessert table at Thanksgiving and Christmas when the boiled custard is served. It contains a flask of Tennessee whiskey, but we just call it "flavoring" as a favor to Mama.

—Cassandra Vanhooser, Associate Livings Editor

Boiled Custard

prep: 15 min.   cook: 25 min.

Boiled custard conjures up thoughts of Christmas in many families. It's a simple delicacy that needs no adornment.

4	cups milk
6	large egg yolks
¾	cup sugar
2	tablespoons cornstarch
Dash of salt	
2	teaspoons vanilla extract

Pour milk into top of a double boiler, and bring water to a boil. Heat milk until tiny bubbles begin to appear around edges of pan. Remove from heat, and set aside.

Beat egg yolks with a wire whisk until frothy. Add sugar, cornstarch, and salt, beating until thickened. Gradually stir about 1 cup hot milk into yolk mixture; add to remaining milk, stirring constantly.

Cook custard mixture in double boiler over low heat, stirring occasionally, 25 minutes or until thickened and a candy thermometer registers 180°. (Do not boil.) Stir in vanilla. Serve warm or cold. **Yield: 4 cups.**

Boiled custard means Christmas in my family. First, it's served formally at the dinner table, but later, leftovers are put on the bottom shelf of the refrigerator in a large bowl with a teacup so that the children can help themselves.

—Virginia Cravens Houston, Former Photo Stylist

Old-Fashioned Vanilla Ice Cream

prep: 10 min.   cook: 30 min.   freeze: 30 min.

6   large eggs, lightly beaten
2⅓   cups sugar
4   cups milk
2   cups half-and-half
¼   teaspoon salt
2½   tablespoons vanilla extract
3   cups whipping cream

Combine first 3 ingredients in a large saucepan; cook over low heat, stirring constantly, 25 to 30 minutes or until mixture thickens and coats a spoon; chill.

Stir in half-and-half and remaining ingredients; pour into freezer container of a 5- or 6-quart hand-turned or electric freezer. Freeze according to manufacturer's instructions.

Serve immediately, or spoon into an airtight container; freeze until firm. **Yield: 3½ quarts.**

I never eat homemade ice cream that I don't remember sitting on the freezer when it got too hard for my dad to crank. He'd put layers of newspapers over the top and cover them with a towel. That was back when "premium" meant the ice cream you licked off the dasher.

—Julie Christopher, Test Kitchens Staff

Chew Cakes

Eloise Long. My grandmother. Working single mother of four big, strong, loud, *hungry* boys, God rest her dear soul.

Grandmother Long was a force to be reckoned with. She raised her sons in a small house on the south side of Atlanta, worked long hours, and came home to fix Southern fare at its finest every night.

As her boys grew up, they brought their own hungry children for lively Sunday afternoon meals and Christmas Eve dinners. We all gathered round to hear them discuss important issues—the changing face of their hometown, jobs lost and found, and, most importantly, SEC football. The topics would vary, the hairlines and waistlines shifted, but one thing never changed: Grandmother Long's cooking. This was the only woman I ever knew who could reduce a red-eye gravy, whip up a batch of fluffy divinity, or pour up a pitcher of tea, all while keeping track of whether it was first and goal or a turnover for her team.

I loved all her cooking, but I was too young when she was around to really appreciate it. My focus was on her kitchen table—that's where she kept the sweets. Any time of year, you could find something good there. At Christmas, it was filled with her legendary treats, most notably her white-as-snow divinity. As a child, the challenge of making divinity wasn't on my radar, but something else was: something she called Chew Cakes. Chew Cakes—part blonde brownie, part brown sugar cake, part heaven. She cut them into long finger-shaped bars and made them without nuts, just for me.

Unfortunately, Grandmother Long's life was cut too short, but her legend has lived on. We found a bunch of splattered recipe cards in her kitchen that sparked a love of baking for my sister, Mary, and me. We tried to re-create many of her famous recipes, especially that of the Chew Cake. We followed the recipe and got dried-out cake. We added more butter, reduced the flour, tried 3 eggs, then 4 eggs. For something seemingly simple, we tried every combination possible with no success. We finally gave up, understanding that our grandmother, a fun-filled, busy woman, had no need or time for the boundaries of a recipe. She made it up as she went. So my sister and I made a silent pact. We agreed to hold the memory of those Chew Cakes in our hearts and minds and let that inspire us to continue her tradition of feeding those around her—with food, with fun, with a life that doesn't always have room for an exact recipe.

—Allison Long Lowery, Managing Editor, Books

Summertime Peach Ice Cream

stand: 1 hr.   prep: 30 min.   freeze: 1 hr., 30 min.

Fragrant ripe (soft) fruit lends the smoothest texture and most pronounced flavor to a purist's dessert like homemade ice cream.

4   cups peeled, diced fresh peaches (about
    8 small ripe peaches)
1   cup sugar
1   (12-ounce) can evaporated milk
1   (3.75-ounce) package vanilla instant pudding
    mix
1   (14-ounce) can sweetened condensed milk
4   cups half-and-half

Combine peaches and sugar, and let stand 1 hour.

Process peach mixture in a food processor until smooth, stopping to scrape down sides.

Stir together evaporated milk and pudding mix in a large bowl; stir in peach purée, sweetened condensed milk, and half-and-half.

Pour peach mixture into freezer container of a 4-quart hand-turned or electric freezer; freeze according to manufacturer's instructions. Spoon into an airtight container, and freeze until firm. **Yield: 2 quarts.**

Classic Cola Float

Classic Cola Float

prep: 2 min.

Add cherry syrup or flavored soda to this kid-friendly quencher. It's even better topped with a maraschino cherry with a stem.

Vanilla ice cream
1 (12-ounce) can cola soft drink
¼ teaspoon vanilla extract

Scoop ice cream into a tall glass, filling half full. Top with cola, and gently stir in vanilla. Serve immediately. **Yield: 1 serving.**

Root Beer Float

prep: 2 min.

Use premium root beer and a high-quality vanilla ice cream to make the best dessert drink.

Vanilla ice cream
1 (12-ounce) can root beer

Scoop ice cream into a tall glass, filling half full. Top with root beer, and gently stir. Serve immediately. **Yield: 1 serving.**

Porter Float

prep: 2 min.

Dark beer gives the ice-cream float a new dimension.

Vanilla ice cream
3 to 4 tablespoons creamy porter or stout beer*
Fresh raspberries
Fresh mint sprig

Scoop ice cream into a tall glass, filling two-thirds full. Top with a few tablespoonfuls of beer. Top with raspberries and a mint sprig. **Yield: 1 serving.**

*For testing purposes only, we tested with Samuel Smith Oatmeal Stout.

Hot Fudge Sundae Shake

prep: 10 min.

A good hot fudge sundae brings out the child in us all. This version takes the sundae to a crazy-good level with brownie chunks and caramel topping. Microwave the caramel and fudge toppings according to package directions. Pick up brownies from your favorite local bakery.

1	pint vanilla bean ice cream*
½	cup milk
8	tablespoons hot fudge topping, warmed*
8	tablespoons caramel topping, warmed*
1	(8.5-ounce) can refrigerated instant whipped cream
¼	cup crumbled brownies, divided
4	maraschino cherries (with stems)

Process ice cream and milk in a blender until smooth, stopping to scrape down sides.
Divide half of ice-cream mixture among 4 (8-ounce) glasses. Top each with 1 tablespoon fudge topping and 1 tablespoon caramel topping. Repeat layers with remaining ice-cream mixture and fudge and caramel toppings.
Top each with instant whipped cream; sprinkle each with 1 tablespoon crumbled brownies, and top with a cherry. Serve immediately. **Yield: 4 servings.**

*For testing purposes only, we used Häagen-Dazs Vanilla Bean Ice Cream and Smucker's Hot Fudge and Caramel-Flavored Toppings.

holidays & special occasions

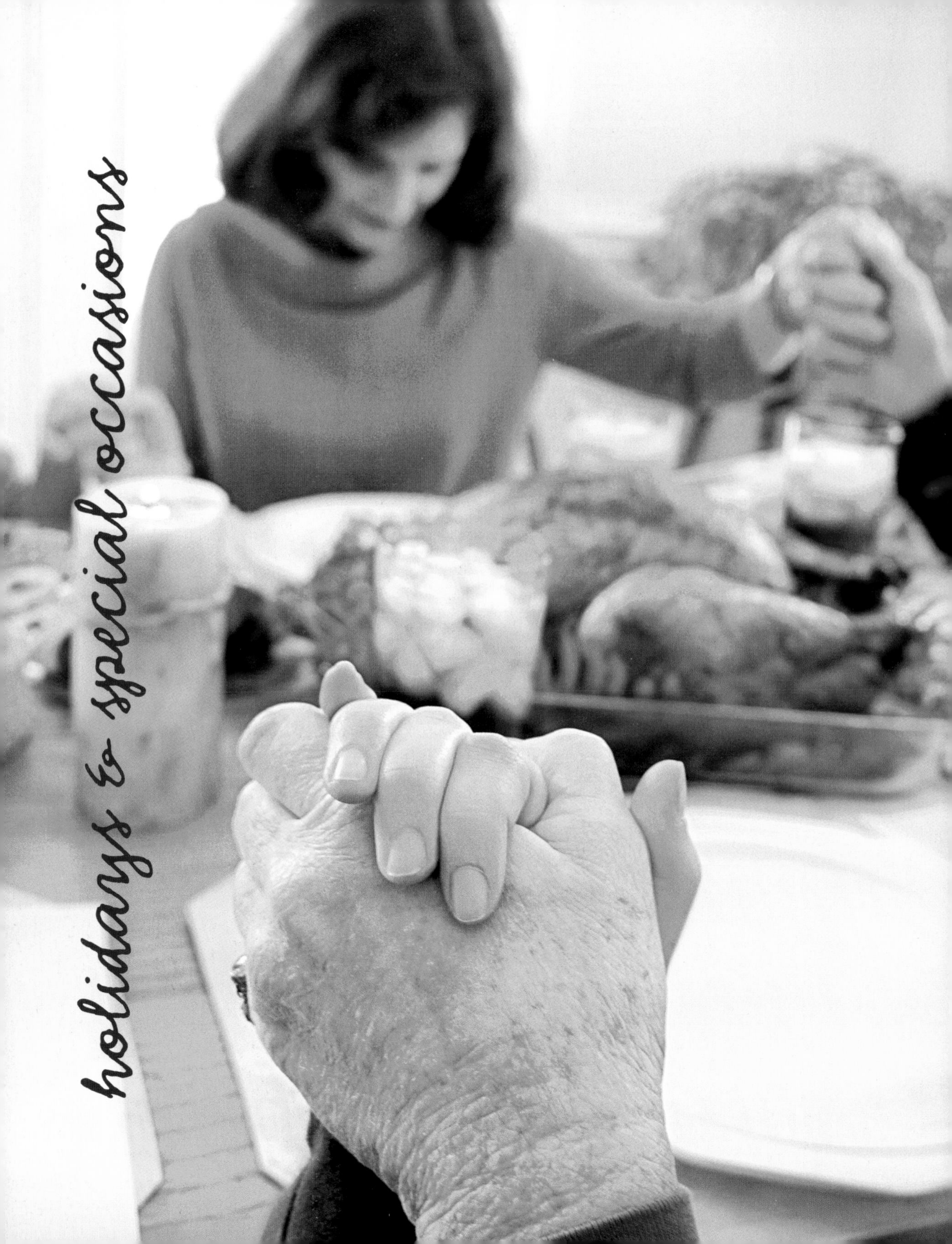

Saying Grace

"Bless this food to the nourishment of our bodies ..."
Every Thanksgiving, when we return thanks before the meal, I realize I look forward to this family ritual as much as I do the holiday feast. I say this with all respect to the fine cooks in the kitchen, but I have learned through the years that it is the blessing that nourishes me long after the turkey is gone.

Like many Southerners, I can trace my father's blessing back to his father, and his father before him, thanks to my great-aunt Myrtle. Myrtle not only remembers every word of her Papaw Tom's original blessing, but she also recalls how food always tasted better when it was blessed. "I'll tell you one thing," she says, "if I ever ate a meal and didn't give thanks, I'd feel like a hog rooting around under an oak tree. He never looks up to see where the acorns came from."

To be sure, gratitude inspires our family's grace-saying, but the remembering also feeds us at this time of year. When my father solemnly bows his head and folds his hands, the familiar words restore a faded picture ...

... The aroma of cornbread dressing wafts under my freckled nose as I stand shrouded in relatives around a dining table in a rural Kentucky farmhouse. Coming through the doorway from the kitchen is my grandmother, her eyes bright, her hair wispy with perspiration. She takes off her apron, looks around to make sure the entire brood is present, then asks, "Milton, will you return thanks?"

Back then, to be asked to say the blessing was an honor that always went to the male head of household, an elder guest, or a visiting preacher. This is still true in many Southern homes. But in keeping with the times, more women and children are being invited to return thanks, with the privilege sometimes going to the youngest.

continued

A friend chuckles over the mealtime trials of her grandfather when he was a rebellious "PK" (preacher's kid) growing up in Mississippi. His father insisted that all the children say a Bible verse for grace at each meal. Whenever the boy's turn came, he stubbornly repeated, "Jesus wept."

Recently, friends of mine fared better when their little girl opted to sing her offering, a rousing version of the Johnny Appleseed song: "The Lord is good to me. So I thank the Lord for giving me the things I need, the sun and the rain and the appleseed...." Not surprisingly, this 4-year-old brought the house down.

When I was growing up, we took turns saying the blessing. A worldly kid, or so I thought, I would rush through a quick list of thank-yous or test my parents' sense of humor with the likes of "God is good, God is great, I hope I get the biggest plate."

Today, I admire someone who can say a good grace. Most of us have at least one in the family. On my husband's side, his brother Bill enjoys a distinct advantage, possessing, as he does, a rich, sonorous voice that flows like a river when he prays. What else makes his grace-saying unique? Part of it comes from the lyrical mixing of the King James English with a Southern drawl. The rest of it comes from the heart. Bill is eloquent, but he is also considerate. He never leaves anyone out, blessing those present, those absent, the house, the food, the hands that prepared the food, and folks I would never think of—being distracted as I am by the smell of Aunt Sarah's hot, buttered rolls.

This Thanksgiving, I will listen again while the blessing is said, savoring my father's comfortable lines and appreciating anew the poise with which he amends them to include relatives who have traveled great distances, the cooks, and the less fortunate.

I am beginning to understand why I need this ritual. As often as we come together around this table, our blessing defines us as a family: who we were and what we are. It's our way of looking up to see where the acorns come from—and giving thanks to the oak tree.

—Jennifer Greer, Contributing Writer and Author of Numerous Books

Simple Turnip Greens

prep: 30 min.   cook: 1 hr., 45 min.

Ring in the New Year with good-luck greens and individual crispy cornbread cakes for sopping up the liquor. Adding sugar to the greens during cooking eliminates any bitter taste.

1	bunch fresh turnip greens (about 4½ pounds)
1	pound salt pork (streak of lean) or smoked pork shoulder
¼	teaspoon freshly ground pepper
2	teaspoons sugar (optional)

Remove and discard stems and discolored spots from greens. Wash greens thoroughly; drain and tear greens into pieces. Set aside.

Slice salt pork at ¼-inch intervals, cutting to, but not through, the skin.

Combine salt pork, 3 quarts water, pepper, and, if desired, sugar in a Dutch oven; bring mixture to a boil. Cover, reduce heat, and simmer 1 hour.

Add greens, and cook, uncovered, 30 to 45 minutes or until tender. Serve with a slotted spoon. **Yield: 4 to 6 servings.**

Hot-Water Cornbread

prep: 5 min.   cook: 6 min. per batch

2	cups white cornmeal
¼	teaspoon baking powder
1¼	teaspoons salt
1	teaspoon sugar
¼	cup half-and-half
1	tablespoon vegetable oil
1	to 2 cups boiling water
Vegetable oil	
Softened butter	

Combine first 4 ingredients in a bowl; stir in half-and-half and 1 tablespoon oil. Gradually add boiling water, stirring until batter is the consistency of grits (see note below).

Pour oil to a depth of ½ inch into a large heavy skillet; place over medium-high heat. Scoop batter into a ¼-cup measure; drop into hot oil, and fry, in batches, 3 minutes on each side or until golden. Drain on paper towels. Serve with softened butter. **Yield: 1 dozen.**

Note: The amount of boiling water needed varies depending on the type of cornmeal used. Stone-ground (coarsely ground) cornmeal requires more liquid.

Hearty Black-eyed Peas

Hearty Black-eyed Peas

prep: 10 min.   cook: 1 hr., 35 min.

Serve these slow-simmered peas plain or with rice and cornbread.

3	cups low-sodium chicken broth
1	medium onion, chopped
1	smoked ham hock
1	bay leaf
½	teaspoon pepper
4	whole jalapeño peppers (optional)
1	(16-ounce) package dried black-eyed peas
1	teaspoon salt

Bring 3 cups water, broth, next 4 ingredients, and, if desired, jalapeños to a boil in a Dutch oven; cover, reduce heat, and simmer 30 minutes.

Rinse and sort peas according to package directions. Add peas and ½ teaspoon salt to Dutch oven, and cook, covered, 1 hour or until peas are tender. If desired, remove meat from ham hock, finely chop, and return to Dutch oven. Season with remaining ½ teaspoon salt or to taste. Remove and discard bay leaf. **Yield: 4 to 6 servings.**

Quick Hoppin' John

prep: 10 min.   cook: 10 min.   stand: 5 min.

This peas-and-rice dish is the ideal accompaniment to pork or ham—and not just on New Year's Day, but year-round.

3	bacon slices, chopped
½	cup chopped celery
⅓	cup chopped onion
1	(15-ounce) can black-eyed peas, undrained
1	cup quick long-grain rice, uncooked
2	tablespoons chopped fresh parsley
½	teaspoon dried thyme

Cook bacon in a large saucepan until crisp, stirring often. Add celery and onion; cook, stirring constantly, until vegetables are tender. **Stir** in 1 cup water and peas; bring to a boil. Cover, reduce heat, and simmer 5 minutes. Stir in rice, parsley, and thyme. Remove from heat; cover and let stand 5 minutes or until liquid is absorbed and rice is tender. **Yield: 2 to 4 servings.**

A Piggy Tale

Food memories have sprinkled my whole life, but the first memorable event happened when I was a small boy. My guess is I was around 7 or 8.

It was a cold November morning, and we came from our tiny concrete-block house in Selma, Alabama, out to Potters Station to help with an annual rite of fall: dressing hogs with my Aunt Jane and Uncle Bob. This included making sausage, cutting pork chops, salt-curing hams, and getting the smokehouse going. The morning always had to be cold and, while I was too young to watch the slaughter, I was in charge of keeping the fire burning high under the iron pot so the water would stay at a boil.

Once the hogs were split and the skin singed, they were dropped quickly into boiling water to remove remaining hair and dirt and clean the skin. I'll spare the exact details, but some 50 years later it is still memorable.

Next, the fun part of the day began for me: making the sausage. The real work was strictly left to the expertise of my Aunt Jane. She would mix her recipe of spices, making sure the amount of sage was just enough and not overpowering for the lean and fat meat from the leftover butchered parts of the hog. Once the meat went through the grinder, her special spice blend was mixed into the ground pork.

After the meat was fed into the casings, I, along

with the other children, got to tie off some of the links. It was neat to see my uncle hang our handiwork in the old smokehouse.

The other half of the mixture was made into patties and frozen in pound-size packages to be cooked as needed. If enough men were present, they would attack cutting the pork chops and loins for freezing with great vigor. While I was much too young to use a knife, in between playing with the fire or tying casings, I would wrap a package or two of the meat.

Of course the hams and shoulders were the prize. Each one was carefully groomed. Shoulders were smoked or salt-cured, but the real delight was freezing them to use for barbecue at the next big family celebration. Hams and bacon, on the other hand, were either cured or smoked. The Morton curing salt was just about the only thing we bought, outside of freezing paper. The ham and bacon slabs were placed in big wooden boxes that looked like feeding troughs with lids and left to cure for weeks. Then they were removed, washed, dried, and put in paper bags and hung so there was good air flow around them. Those that we smoked seemed to never get ready.

Day after day, the aroma filled the air whenever we stopped to visit over the next month. Finally the first prized and biggest ham was served at my aunt and uncle's home to all who helped make the cold Saturday a success and provide pork for their table all winter.

—John Alex Floyd, Jr., Editor in Chief

A Father's Gift

The smell of country ham on winter wind perfumes all of my Christmas memories. Daddy approached the ham with the seriousness of a surgeon, first amputating the hock and setting it aside to be used later to season the beans and greens. Then he'd trim the edges so that the ham was the exact size of my grandmother's roasting pan, borrowed for this special occasion.

Daddy added a molasses concoction, the recipe for which he took to his grave, never having revealed exactly what he used. When he deemed the ham done, he'd bring it inside and allow each of us a tiny sample before hiding it away.

On Christmas day, the country ham was always the last dish to come to the table. It was a meal that was months in the making.

Even today, when I serve the Christmas ham, I think of my father. As far as I know, he never gave me a store-bought gift. A busy farmer with many mouths to feed, he left those duties to my mother. But during this Christmas ritual, he shared his wit and wisdom, along with this priceless lesson: When you give of yourself, it means more than any store-bought present ever could.

—Cassandra Vanhooser, Associate Livings Editor

Holiday Ham

prep: 25 min.   bake: 2 hr., 30 min.

Baked ham is great to have on hand during the holidays. Use it to make Ham-and-Dijon Biscuits on page 254, or serve it for breakfast along with hot biscuits, cheese grits, and fresh fruit.

1   (8- to 10-pound) fully cooked, bone-in ham
1   (0.62-ounce) jar whole cloves
1   (16-ounce) package dark brown sugar
1   cup spicy brown mustard
1   cup apple cider
½   cup bourbon
1   cup hot brewed coffee (optional)
Garnishes: fresh rosemary, fresh sage, orange wedges

Preheat oven to 350°. Remove skin from ham, and trim fat to ¼-inch thickness. Make shallow cuts in fat in a diamond pattern. Push cloves into ham in a decorative pattern; place ham in a lightly greased roasting pan or 13- x 9-inch pan.
Stir together brown sugar and next 3 ingredients. Pour mixture over ham.
Bake at 350° on lower oven rack for 2 to 2½ hours or until a meat thermometer inserted into thickest portion registers 140°, basting with pan juices every 20 minutes. Shield ham after 1½ hours to prevent excessive browning, if necessary. Remove ham to a serving platter, and let cool.
Meanwhile, if desired, stir coffee into drippings to loosen browned particles in pan. Pour drippings into a saucepan, and cook 5 to 8 minutes or until slightly thickened. Serve sauce with ham. Garnish ham platter, if desired. Cover and store ham and sauce separately in refrigerator for up to 5 days. **Yield: 12 servings.**

Tomato Aspic

prep: 30 min.   cook: 5 min.   chill: 3 hr., 30 min.

Tomato aspic is known as the perfect fare for a ladies' luncheon or a spring brunch. Check your grandmother's cabinets for vintage aspic molds.

3	envelopes unflavored gelatin
4	cups tomato juice, divided
1	tablespoon prepared horseradish
2	teaspoons Worcestershire sauce
1	teaspoon hot sauce
½	teaspoon celery salt
⅔	cup finely chopped green bell pepper
⅔	cup finely chopped celery
1	tablespoon plus 1 teaspoon grated onion
1	medium cucumber

Curly leaf lettuce

Sprinkle gelatin over 1 cup tomato juice in a medium saucepan; let stand 1 minute. Cook over medium heat, stirring constantly, 3 to 5 minutes or until gelatin dissolves. Remove from heat; transfer mixture to a large bowl.

Stir in remaining 3 cups tomato juice, horseradish, and next 3 ingredients. Chill mixture to the consistency of unbeaten egg whites. Fold in bell pepper, celery, and onion. Spoon tomato mixture into eight lightly oiled individual ½-cup molds. Cover and chill at least 3 hours or until firm.

Score cucumber with tines of a fork. Thinly slice cucumber. Place lettuce leaves on individual salad plates or on 2 large pedestals, and arrange cucumber slices in a circle over lettuce leaves.

Unmold salads onto prepared plates or pedestals. **Yield: 8 servings.**

Sally's Cheese Straws

prep: 15 min.   cook: 10 min. per batch

1   (16-ounce) block sharp Cheddar cheese,
    shredded (not preshredded), at room
    temperature
1½ cups all-purpose flour
¼   cup butter, softened
1   teaspoon salt
¼   teaspoon ground red pepper
⅛   teaspoon dry mustard

Process all ingredients in a food processor
about 30 seconds or until mixture forms a ball.
Preheat oven to 375°. Fit a cookie press with a
bar-shaped disk, and shape dough into straws,
following manufacturer's instructions, on
ungreased baking sheets. Cut ribbons crosswise with a knife to make individual straws.
Bake at 375° for 8 to 10 minutes or until lightly
browned. Transfer to wire racks to cool. **Yield:
about 8 dozen.**

Curried Chicken Salad Tea Sandwiches

prep: 1 hr.

Tea sandwiches like these (as well as ham biscuits) display beautifully on tiered plates topped with a small bouquet of flowers for a wedding day menu (see page 255 for inspiration).

4	cups finely chopped cooked chicken
3	(8-ounce) packages cream cheese, softened
¾	cup dried cranberries, chopped
½	cup sweetened flaked coconut, toasted
6	green onions, minced
2	celery ribs, diced
1	(2¼-ounce) package slivered almonds, toasted
1	tablespoon curry powder
1	tablespoon freshly grated ginger
½	teaspoon salt
½	teaspoon pepper
48	whole-grain bread slices

Stir together first 11 ingredients. Spread mixture on 1 side each of 24 bread slices; top with remaining 24 bread slices. Trim crusts from sandwiches; cut each sandwich into 4 rectangles with a serrated knife. **Yield: about 25 servings.**

Ham-and-Dijon Biscuits With Caramelized Onion Butter

prep: 17 min.   bake: 15 min. per batch

These Southern ham biscuits certainly qualify as wedding reception worthy, but they're equally at home on a holiday sideboard. We recommend using Holiday Ham (page 248) for this recipe. You can also use any baked ham or even thinly sliced ham from the deli.

9   cups all-purpose baking mix
2   cups milk
½   cup Dijon mustard
¼   cup honey
Caramelized Onion Butter
Ham (about 2 pounds)

Preheat oven to 450°. Make a well in center of baking mix in a large bowl.

Whisk together milk, mustard, and honey. Add milk mixture to baking mix, stirring just until moistened.

Turn out soft dough onto a floured surface; knead 3 or 4 times.

Roll half of dough at a time to ½-inch thickness; cut with a 2-inch round cutter, and place on lightly greased baking sheets. Reroll dough and cut scraps.

Bake at 450° for 8 minutes or until lightly browned. Split warm biscuits. Spread with Caramelized Onion Butter, and fill with slivers of ham. Cover biscuits loosely with aluminum foil. **Reduce** oven temperature to 350°. Bake at 350° for 5 to 7 minutes or just until thoroughly heated. **Yield: 4 dozen.**

Note: To make ahead, place assembled biscuits in an airtight container, and chill up to 8 hours or freeze up to 3 weeks. Thaw frozen biscuits in refrigerator. To reheat, place biscuits on baking sheets, and cover loosely with aluminum foil. Bake at 350° for 10 to 12 minutes or until heated.

Caramelized Onion Butter

prep: 5 min.   cook: 20 min.

1¾   cups butter, softened and divided
2   large sweet onions, finely chopped
¼   cup firmly packed brown sugar
1   tablespoon balsamic vinegar

Melt ¼ cup butter over medium-high heat in a large skillet. Add onions and brown sugar, and cook, stirring often, 15 to 20 minutes or until a deep caramel color. Remove from heat; cool slightly. Stir in remaining 1½ cups butter and vinegar. Use in recipe above, or cover and chill. Return to room temperature before serving. **Yield: 2½ cups.**

Birthday Cake

prep: 15 min.   bake: 30 min.   cool: 25 min.   freeze: 4 hr.   stand: 2 hr.

This recipe bakes up into a really tender three-layer white cake. (Freezing the layers before frosting them makes assembly easy.) It's an ideal birthday cake for young ones.

½   cup butter, softened
½   cup shortening
2   cups sugar
3   cups cake flour
4   teaspoons baking powder
½   teaspoon salt
⅔   cup milk
2   teaspoons vanilla extract
¾   teaspoon almond extract
6   egg whites
Milk Chocolate Frosting
Garnish: multicolored candy sprinkles

Preheat oven to 325°. Beat butter and shortening at medium speed with an electric mixer until creamy; gradually add sugar, beating well. **Combine** flour, baking powder, and salt; add to butter mixture alternately with milk and ⅔ cup water, beginning and ending with flour mixture.

Beat at low speed until blended after each addition. Stir in extracts.

Beat egg whites at high speed with electric mixer until stiff peaks form; fold about one-third of egg whites into batter. Gradually fold in remaining egg whites. Pour cake batter into 3 greased and floured 8-inch round cake pans.

Bake at 325° for 25 to 30 minutes or until a wooden pick inserted in center comes out clean. Cool in pans on wire racks 10 minutes. Remove from pans to wire racks, and let cool 15 minutes. Wrap each layer in plastic wrap. Freeze 4 hours.

Unwrap frozen cake layers. Spread Milk Chocolate Frosting between layers and on top and sides of cake. Let stand at room temperature 2 hours before serving. Garnish, if desired. **Yield: 12 servings.**

Milk Chocolate Frosting

prep: 10 min.

1   cup butter, softened
6   cups powdered sugar
⅓   cup unsweetened cocoa
½   cup milk

Beat butter at medium speed with an electric mixer until creamy. Add remaining ingredients, beating until smooth. **Yield: 4 cups.**

Homemade Limeade

prep: 20 min.   chill: 8 hr.

For a fun garnish, thread lime slices on wooden skewers and float the skewers in the pitcher or in tall glasses.

1½ cups sugar
½   cup boiling water
2   teaspoons lime zest
1½ cups fresh lime juice (10 to 14 limes)
5   cups cold water
Garnishes: lime slices, fresh mint sprigs

Stir together sugar and boiling water until sugar dissolves.
Stir in lime zest, lime juice, and cold water. Chill 8 hours. Garnish, if desired. **Yield: 8 cups.**

Note: To make Homemade Lemonade, substitute lemon zest and lemon juice for lime zest and lime juice.

The Fourth of July is as big as Christmas at my house. I shop for this day all year long. When guests arrive for the annual backyard breakfast, they find a table with a card that reads, "Sign in and eat up!"

—Margaret Hathaway, *Southern Living* Reader

Patriotic Cupcakes

prep: 40 min.   bake: 22 min.   cool: 55 min.

Spreading frosting on cupcakes can be time-consuming. You'll love our quick-and-easy technique using a zip-top plastic freezer bag.

2   cups sugar
1   cup butter, softened
2   large eggs
2   teaspoons fresh lemon juice
1   teaspoon vanilla extract
2½   cups cake flour
½   teaspoon baking soda
1   cup buttermilk
24   paper baking cups
5-Cup Cream Cheese Frosting (page 195)
24 miniature American flags

Preheat oven to 350°. Beat sugar and butter at medium speed with an electric mixer until creamy. Add eggs, 1 at a time, beating until yellow disappears after each addition. Beat in lemon juice and vanilla.

Combine flour and baking soda in a small bowl; add to sugar mixture alternately with buttermilk, beginning and ending with flour mixture. Beat at medium speed just until blended after each addition.

Place 24 paper baking cups in muffin pans. Spoon batter into baking cups, filling two-thirds full.

Bake at 350° for 18 to 22 minutes or until a wooden pick inserted in center comes out clean. Cool in pans on a wire rack 10 minutes. Remove cupcakes from pans to wire rack, and cool 45 minutes or until completely cool.

Spoon 5-Cup Cream Cheese Frosting into a zip-top plastic freezer bag (do not seal). Snip 1 corner of bag to make a hole (about 1 inch in diameter). Pipe frosting in little loops onto tops of cupcakes as desired. Insert 1 flag into top of each cupcake. **Yield: 2 dozen.**

Note: To make ahead, bake and cool cupcakes as directed. Do not frost and decorate. Double-wrap cupcakes in plastic wrap and heavy-duty aluminum foil or place in airtight containers, and freeze up to 1 month.

Behold the Barbecue Sundae

Perhaps my most powerful comfort food memory centers around something called a barbecue sundae. In fact, when combined with the nostalgic, happy-sad tug of fall weather, the emotions surrounding this unique food are pegged right about DEFCON 1. I've been caught by my girls sitting on our back porch, eyes closed as I transport myself back to Oxford, Mississippi, and a spot called the Rebel Barn to make it all better. They look at me as if I've lost my mind (and maybe I have), but I know it's one of my culinary happy places. For it was there, in that tiny drive-thru convenience store, that this magical concoction of goodness was created.

The curative powers of a barbecue sundae are legendary among the Ole Miss faithful. Layers of succulent pulled pork, creamy slaw, and tangy baked beans piled high in a Styrofoam cup warmed my soul and bolstered my spirit on crisp, college football Saturdays. Standard pregame operating procedure called for loading in the back of a buddy's pickup early to make our way to the Barn. The queue of vehicles could be substantial, but finally getting a sundae was like reaching the pot of gold at the end of a rainbow.

These days, regardless of the season, my wife and I often celebrate and entertain with this multilevel delight. It's quite simply barbecue (and emotional) therapy at its finest.

—Scott Jones, Executive Food Editor

Barbecue Sundae

prep: 10 min.

Pick up the elements for this savory sundae at a local meat-and-three or your favorite barbecue joint.

2   cups warm baked beans
2   cups coleslaw
1   pound warm shredded barbecued pork
Barbecue sauce
Dill pickle wedges (optional)

Divide baked beans among 4 small bowls, mugs, or wide-mouth jars; top each portion of beans with ½ cup coleslaw, ¼ pound warm shredded barbecued pork, and sauce. Serve with a dill pickle wedge, if desired. **Yield: 4 servings.**

Root Beer Baked Beans

prep: 5 min.   cook: 12 min.   bake: 55 min.

You don't taste the root beer in this recipe; it's just used for sweetening instead of the traditional brown sugar.

3   bacon slices
1   small onion, diced
2   (16-ounce) cans pork and beans
½   cup root beer (not diet)
¼   cup hickory-smoked barbecue sauce
½   teaspoon dry mustard
⅛   teaspoon hot sauce

Preheat oven to 400°. Cook bacon in a skillet over medium heat until crisp; remove and drain on paper towels, reserving 2 tablespoons drippings in skillet. Crumble bacon.
Sauté diced onion in hot bacon drippings in skillet over high heat 5 minutes or until tender. Stir together onion, crumbled bacon, beans, and remaining ingredients in a greased 1-quart baking dish.
Bake beans, uncovered, at 400° for 55 minutes or until thickened. **Yield: 4 servings.**

Caramel Apples

Caramel Apples

prep: 20 min.   chill: 15 min.

Caramel apples are the stuff of fall festivals and Halloween carnivals. No doubt, with each messy bite, they bring out the child in us all.

6   large Granny Smith apples
6   wooden craft sticks
1   (14-ounce) bag caramels, unwrapped*
1   tablespoon vanilla extract
2   cups chopped pecans or peanuts, toasted
1   (12-ounce) bag semisweet chocolate morsels
     (optional)
Pecan halves (optional)

Wash and dry apples; remove stems. Insert a craft stick into stem end of each apple; set aside.

Combine caramels, vanilla, and 1 tablespoon water in a microwave-safe glass bowl. Microwave at HIGH 90 seconds or until melted, stirring twice.

Dip each apple into the caramel mixture quickly, allowing excess caramel to drip off. Roll in chopped nuts; place apples on lightly greased wax paper. Chill at least 15 minutes.

If desired, to make chocolate-dipped caramel apples, microwave chocolate morsels at HIGH 90 seconds or until melted, stirring twice; cool 5 minutes. Pour chocolate where craft sticks and apples meet, allowing chocolate to drip down sides of caramel apples. Press pecan halves onto chocolate, if desired. Chill 15 minutes or until set. **Yield: 6 apples.**

*For testing purposes only, we used Kraft Caramels.

Popcorn Balls

prep: 20 min.

30   marshmallows
¼   cup butter
10   cups fresh popped popcorn (¾ cup popcorn
      kernels)
1½   cups candy-coated chocolate pieces

Melt marshmallows and butter in a saucepan over low heat. Pour over popcorn in a large bowl, and toss to coat. Gently stir in chocolate pieces. Shape into 4-inch balls. Cool slightly, and wrap each in plastic wrap. Store in an airtight container. **Yield: 16 popcorn balls.**

Cornbread Dressing

Making your first cornbread dressing is a rite of passage, something you just want to be able to do so your mama can feel good about your upbringing.

The ingredients you use say something about you. Cooks from coastal areas are likely to stir in seafood. Sausage is added in many locales. And you can argue over whether cornbread, biscuits, or store-bought stuffing mix works best as a base. I guess that's what I found intimidating. All those special twists made it seem impossible for a rookie like me to pull it off.

Eventually, however, I decided to find a classic recipe, put aside my fear of excessive sage, and give it a try. I picked one with a cornbread base.

It's actually relatively easy to make. Most of the required ingredients were already in my cupboard, and none of them was expensive.

What I loved most about making dressing was that it made my kitchen smell like my mother's. Whenever there was dressing on the table, I was surrounded by people I loved. I can't think of a better reason to make it.

—Valerie Fraser Luesse,
Creative Development Director

Roast Turkey and Gravy

prep: 14 min.   bake: 2 hr., 50 min.   cook: 7 min.

1   (12- to 14-pound) turkey
1   tablespoon salt
2   teaspoons pepper
½   cup butter, softened
1   Golden Delicious apple, quartered
1   large yellow onion, quartered
2   large carrots, cut into 3-inch pieces
3   celery ribs with leaves, cut into 3-inch pieces
4   cups hot water
⅓   cup all-purpose flour
Cornbread Dressing (page 269)

Preheat oven to 425°. Remove giblets and neck from turkey; rinse and reserve for another use. **Rinse** turkey with cold water, and pat dry. Sprinkle cavity with ½ tablespoon salt and 1 teaspoon pepper. Rub skin of turkey with butter, and sprinkle with remaining ½ tablespoon salt and 1 teaspoon pepper.
Place apple, onion, carrot, and celery in turkey cavity. Lift wingtips up and over back, and tuck under bird. Place turkey, breast side up, on a lightly greased rack in a roasting pan.
Bake at 425° on lower oven rack 20 minutes. Reduce oven temperature to 325°. Add hot water to pan, and bake 2 to 2½ hours or until a meat thermometer inserted in turkey thigh registers 170°, shielding turkey with foil after 1 hour and basting with pan juices every 20 minutes. Let stand 15 minutes. Transfer to a serving platter; reserve 2½ cups drippings.
Whisk together drippings and ⅓ cup flour in a medium saucepan. Cook over medium heat, whisking constantly, 5 to 7 minutes or until thick and bubbly. Season gravy to taste. Serve gravy with Cornbread Dressing and turkey.
Yield: 12 to 14 servings.

To Grandmother's House We Went

Forty years ago, when I was a small child growing up in the Deep South, the bounty and splendor of our holiday dinners were rivaled only by the food pavilion at the state fair. Our family would gather at my grandmother's house for an enormous midday meal. The ancient dining table groaned beneath the weight of huge silver platters overflowing with roasted turkey and hickory-smoked ham. The ham was always glazed a bright mahogany red, with brown sugar and bourbon (a secret ingredient kept hidden beneath some loosened floorboards in the kitchen closet).

My grandmother, Mamere, lived in a rambling old farmhouse she shared with Olivia, her longtime cook and traveling companion. Its long side porch overlooked the pond where the wild geese wintered. Mamere believed that porches were magical places and that, like still waters and green pastures, they held the power to comfort and restore the soul. It was a place of a hundred small celebrations that surrounded the coming and going of more formal holidays.

On Christmas Eve, Olivia and Mamere hosted a children's party and decorated the porch with miniature trees wrapped in garlands of sugarplums. Warmed with cocoa and quilts, we would nestle in the swing cushions and listen for the elusive sound of sleigh bells until we fell asleep and our fathers came to carry us home.

The porch was filled with the smell of honeysuckle and wood smoke—an aroma signaling the advent of Olivia's holiday baking in the porch's wood-burning stove. It was a yearly ritual that began with a dozen batches of shortbread and culminated with a magnificent charlotte russe on Christmas Day.

It all made for a series of glorious and merry feasts with as many relatives and stories as there were recipes. In the afternoon, when the last morsel was finished, the men migrated from their dining room chairs to the side porch, spinning tales of fishing and football glories.

Over the years, our family has grown with new generations. The bounty and splendor of our holiday dinners are often governed by our hectic work schedules and the distance between the cities that now separate us—though we are all certain to have Olivia's ham and Mamere's asparagus casserole. And always, there are the stories that tell of eccentric relatives and old farmhouses, and clear, cold nights on the edge of winter, when small children fell asleep in a porch swing, listening to the sound of sleigh bells very distant and far away.

—**Mary Allen Perry, Associate Food Editor**

Cornbread Dressing

prep: 15 min.   bake: 1 hr., 10 min.

This Southern classic is a Thanksgiving dinner favorite. This version is quite moist;
if you prefer a firmer dressing, use only four cans of broth.

1	cup butter, divided
3	cups white cornmeal
1	cup all-purpose flour
2	tablespoons sugar
2	teaspoons baking powder
1½	teaspoons salt
1	teaspoon baking soda
7	large eggs
3	cups buttermilk
3	cups soft breadcrumbs
3	cups finely chopped celery
2	cups finely chopped onion
½	cup finely chopped fresh sage or 1 tablespoon dried rubbed sage
5	(10½-ounce) cans condensed chicken broth, undiluted
1	tablespoon freshly ground pepper

Preheat oven to 425°. Place ½ cup butter in a 13- x 9-inch pan; heat in oven at 425° for 4 minutes.

Combine cornmeal and next 5 ingredients; whisk in 3 eggs and buttermilk.

Pour hot butter from pan into batter, stirring until blended. Pour batter into pan.

Bake at 425° for 30 minutes or until golden brown. Cool.

Crumble cornbread into a large bowl; stir in breadcrumbs, and set aside.

Melt remaining ½ cup butter in a large skillet over medium heat; add celery and onion, and sauté until tender. Stir in sage, and sauté 1 more minute.

Stir vegetables, remaining 4 eggs, chicken broth, and pepper into cornbread mixture; spoon into 1 lightly greased 13- x 9-inch baking dish and 1 lightly greased 8-inch square baking dish. Cover and chill 8 hours, if desired.

Preheat oven to 375°. Bake dressing, uncovered, at 375° for 35 to 40 minutes or until golden brown. **Yield: 16 to 18 servings.**

For a special presentation, chill the cranberry salad in individual teacups. This works particularly well for holiday luncheons.

—Mary Allen Perry, Associate Food Editor

Fresh Cranberry Congealed Salad

prep: 30 min. chill: 8 hr., 30 min.

1 (12-ounce) package fresh cranberries
½ cup sugar
3 (3-ounce) packages raspberry-flavored gelatin
2 cups boiling water
2 cups cranberry juice, chilled
1 (8-ounce) can crushed pineapple, undrained
2 celery ribs, diced (1 cup)
⅔ cup chopped pecans, toasted
Lettuce leaves
Garnishes: fresh cranberries, fresh mint sprigs

Process cranberries in a food processor 30 seconds or until coarsely chopped, stopping once to scrape down sides.

Stir together cranberries and sugar in a bowl; set aside.

Stir together gelatin and boiling water in a large bowl 2 minutes or until gelatin dissolves. Add juice, and chill 30 minutes or until consistency of unbeaten egg whites.

Stir in cranberry mixture, pineapple, celery, and pecans. Spoon mixture into a lightly greased 10-cup Bundt pan; cover and chill 8 hours or until firm.

Unmold salad onto a lettuce-lined platter. Garnish, if desired. **Yield: 12 servings.**

A Sentimental Journey

I watch her do it every year. Mom leafs through files, shuffles through kitchen drawers, and finally emerges victorious with a handful of old, dog-eared recipes for the dishes our family always expects on the table every Thanksgiving and Christmas. This disorganization isn't a sign of an untidy housekeeper; like every good Southern cook, she's showing respect for family history. After all, if all those odd-size, yellowing slips of paper scrawled by relatives and friends were transcribed to fresh, white index cards, the charm and character would be lost.

Anyway, we all know that how the food tastes isn't as important as who prepared it or how long it has been a tradition when it comes to holidays. Mostly we want the same things year after year so we can reminisce. We bait newcomers or youngsters with a bite of Aunt Martha's famous pie and just wait for them to ask, "Now, what's this called?" and, "So who was she?" Then they're hooked into a line of "remember when" stories they'll find themselves telling years from now.

—Dana Adkins Campbell, Food Editor, 1963–2003

Refrigerator Yeast Rolls

prep: 18 min.   chill: 8 hr.   rise: 45 min.   bake: 14 min.

You may know these as Parker House rolls, but whatever the name, they are classic buttery, soft, folded dinner rolls for any night of the week.

1   (¼-ounce) envelope active dry yeast
2   cups warm water (100° to 110°)
6   cups bread flour
½   cup sugar
2   teaspoons salt
½   cup shortening
2   large eggs, lightly beaten
½   cup butter, melted

Stir together yeast and warm water in a medium bowl; let stand 5 minutes.

Stir together flour, sugar, and salt in a large bowl.

Cut shortening into flour mixture with a pastry blender until crumbly; stir in yeast mixture and eggs just until blended. (Do not overmix.) Cover and chill 8 hours.

Roll dough to ¼-inch thickness on a well-floured surface (dough will be soft); cut with a 2½-inch round cutter.

Brush rounds with melted butter. Make a crease across each round with the dull edge of a knife, and fold in half; gently press edges to seal. Place rolls in a greased 15- x 10-inch jelly-roll pan with sides touching or in 2 (9-inch) square pans. Cover and let rise in a warm place (85°), free from drafts, 45 minutes or until doubled in bulk.

Preheat oven to 400°. Bake at 400° for 14 minutes or until golden. **Yield: about 3 dozen.**

Pumpkin Chess Pie

prep: 15 min.   bake: 1 hr., 10 min.   chill: 8 hr.

Pumpkin pie is traditionally served around the holidays, but this version with its luscious sauce is so good you'll want to serve it year-round.

½   (15-ounce) package refrigerated piecrusts
1   (15-ounce) can unsweetened pumpkin
2   cups sugar
½   cup butter, softened
3   large eggs
½   cup half-and-half
1½ teaspoons vanilla extract
¾   teaspoon salt
½   teaspoon ground cinnamon
¼   teaspoon ground ginger
¼   teaspoon ground cloves
Praline Sauce

Preheat oven to 350°. Fit piecrust in a 9-inch pie plate according to package directions; fold edges under, and crimp.

Beat pumpkin, sugar, and butter in a large bowl at medium speed with an electric mixer until smooth. Add eggs and next 6 ingredients, beating until blended. Pour filling into prepared crust.

Bake at 350° for 1 hour and 10 minutes or until almost set. Cool pie completely on a wire rack. Chill for 8 hours. Serve with Praline Sauce. **Yield: 8 servings.**

Praline Sauce

prep: 5 min.   cook: 1 min.

This rich sauce is also good spooned over ice cream and makes a perfect holiday gift.

1   cup firmly packed brown sugar
½   cup half-and-half
½   cup butter
½   cup chopped pecans, toasted
½   teaspoon vanilla extract

Combine first 3 ingredients in a small saucepan over medium heat. Bring to a boil; cook, stirring constantly, 1 minute. Remove from heat; stir in pecans and vanilla. Cool completely. **Yield: about 2 cups.**

Roasted Pecan Fudge

prep: 15 min.   soak: 20 min.   stand: 1 hr., 30 min.

Pair this creamy, rich chocolate fudge with Peanut Butter Fudge (recipe follows) in a tin for gift giving.

2½ cups pecan halves
4   tablespoons salt
1⅔ cups sugar
⅔   cup evaporated milk
2   tablespoons butter
2   cups miniature marshmallows
1½ cups semisweet chocolate morsels
2   teaspoons vanilla extract

Preheat oven to 450°. Soak pecan halves in water to cover 20 minutes; drain well. Sprinkle 2 tablespoons salt over bottom of a 15- x 10-inch jelly-roll pan. Arrange pecans in a single layer in pan; sprinkle with 2 more tablespoons salt. Place pecans in hot oven, and turn off oven. Let stand in oven 1 hour and 30 minutes. Toss pecans in a strainer to remove excess salt. Coarsely chop pecans, and cool.

Bring sugar, evaporated milk, and butter to a boil in a large heavy saucepan over medium heat; boil, stirring constantly, until a candy thermometer registers 234° (about 7 minutes). **Remove** from heat; stir in marshmallows and chocolate morsels until smooth. Stir in 2 teaspoons vanilla and chopped pecans. **Pour** fudge into a buttered 8-inch square pan, and cool completely. Cut into squares. **Yield: 5 dozen pieces.**

Note: Soft-ball stage (234°) is a candy-making term. Drop a small amount of boiling mixture (in this recipe, the sugar, milk, and butter combination) into a glass cup of cold water. When it forms a soft ball that flattens as you remove it from the water, you've reached the soft-ball stage.

Peanut Butter Fudge

prep: 10 min.   cook: 10 min.   cool: 1 hr.

1   (5-ounce) can evaporated milk
1⅔ cups sugar
½   teaspoon salt
1¾ cups miniature marshmallows
1   (10-ounce) package peanut butter morsels
1   teaspoon vanilla extract
½   cup chopped peanuts

Bring first 3 ingredients to a boil in a large saucepan over medium-high heat. Reduce heat to medium, and cook, stirring constantly, 5 minutes; remove from heat. Add marshmallows, peanut butter morsels, and vanilla; stir until smooth. Pour fudge into a greased 8-inch square pan. Gently press peanuts into top of warm fudge. Let cool 1 hour or until completely cool. Cut into squares. **Yield: 3 dozen pieces.**

Chocolate-Almond
Macaroons

Chocolate-Almond Macaroons

prep: 15 min.   bake: 17 min. per batch

Take time to bake some sweets with your children during the holiday season. Recipes like this for macaroons give kids a chance to take part and create kitchen memories.

¾ cup sweetened condensed milk
1   (14-ounce) package sweetened flaked
    coconut
¼ to ½ teaspoon almond extract
⅛ teaspoon salt
24 whole almonds
½ cup dark chocolate morsels (optional)

Preheat oven to 350°. Stir together first 4 ingredients. Drop dough by lightly greased tablespoonfuls onto parchment paper-lined baking sheets. Gently press an almond into top of each cookie.

Bake at 350° for 15 to 17 minutes or until golden. Remove to wire racks to cool.

If desired, microwave chocolate morsels in a microwave-safe bowl at HIGH 1 minute and 15 seconds or until melted and smooth, stirring every 30 seconds. Transfer to a 1-quart zip-top plastic freezer bag; snip a tiny hole in 1 corner of bag. Pipe melted chocolate over cooled cookies by gently squeezing bag. **Yield: 2 dozen.**

Mrs. Floyd's Divinity

prep: 30 min.   cook: 20 min.

2½ cups sugar
½   cup light corn syrup
¼   teaspoon salt
2   egg whites
1   teaspoon vanilla extract
1   cup chopped pecans, toasted
Garnish: toasted pecan halves

Cook first 3 ingredients with ½ cup water in a heavy 2-quart saucepan over low heat until sugar dissolves and a candy thermometer registers 248° (about 15 minutes). Remove syrup from heat.

Beat egg whites at high speed with an electric mixer until stiff peaks form. Pour half of hot syrup in a thin stream over egg whites, beating constantly at high speed, about 5 minutes.

Cook remaining half of syrup over medium heat, stirring occasionally, until candy thermometer registers 272° (about 4 to 5 minutes). Slowly pour hot syrup and vanilla extract over egg white mixture, beating constantly at high speed until mixture holds its shape (about 6 to 8 minutes). Stir in 1 cup chopped pecans.

Drop mixture quickly by rounded teaspoonfuls onto lightly greased wax paper. Garnish, if desired. Cool. **Yield: 4 dozen (1¾ pounds).**

Walter's Pecan Pie

prep: 5 min.   bake: 40 min.

Chef Walter Royal of The Angus Barn in Raleigh, North Carolina, treats his customers to this fine holiday comfort fare. His pie received our staff's highest rating.

½   (15-ounce) package refrigerated piecrusts
3   large eggs
½   cup sugar
¼   teaspoon salt
3   tablespoons butter, melted
1   cup dark corn syrup
1   teaspoon vanilla extract
2   cups pecan halves

Preheat oven to 350°. Fit piecrust into a 9-inch pie plate according to package directions. Fold edges under, and crimp.

Whisk together eggs and next 5 ingredients until thoroughly blended. Stir in pecans. Pour filling into piecrust.

Bake at 350° on lower rack 40 minutes or until pie is set, shielding edges with aluminum foil after 15 minutes. Cool completely on a wire rack. Serve with vanilla ice cream, if desired. **Yield: 6 servings.**

Christmas Cheer

My Aunt Kat has a secret family eggnog recipe. The family has served it proudly every Christmas since she was a little girl. Her mother, my grandmother Lillie, made it in generous amounts for all the friends and relatives who always dropped in during the holidays. As a younger woman, though, Grandmother Lillie believed that eggnog was a sinful potion.

Aunt Kat loves to tell the story of the first Christmas Grandmother spent with her husband's family. Lillie came from a long line of Baptist ministers who preached against the evils of alcohol. She was shocked when her father-in-law pulled a jug of bourbon from the mahogany sideboard in the dining room. When he poured the whiskey into the cut-glass punch bowl of eggnog, Lillie fainted with fear. When she came to, she was lovingly presented a small cup of the very same eggnog.

Aunt Kat laughs and says, "After that, Mother never did serve eggnog without the bourbon. And you can be sure if Christmas was at Aunt Oma's, it would always have an extra-generous portion of whiskey, which just added to our Christmas cheer!"

—Jan Moon, Former Test Kitchens Professional

Southern Eggnog

prep: 10 min.   cook: 20 min.   chill: 24 hr.

Eggnog, the beloved Christmas beverage, is a cherished Southern tradition—with or without the bourbon.

1	quart milk
4	large eggs
1	cup sugar
2	teaspoons vanilla extract
¼	teaspoon salt
⅔	cup bourbon*

Cook milk in a heavy nonaluminum saucepan over medium heat, stirring often, 10 minutes or just until it begins to steam. (Do not boil.) Remove from heat.

Whisk together eggs and next 3 ingredients until blended. Gradually whisk 1 cup hot milk into egg mixture; whisk egg mixture into remaining hot milk.

Cook over medium heat, stirring constantly, 8 to 10 minutes or until a candy thermometer registers between 170° and 180°. (Do not boil.)

Remove from heat, and pour custard through a fine wire-mesh strainer into a bowl. Place heavy-duty plastic wrap directly on warm custard (to prevent a film from forming), and chill at least 24 hours or up to 3 days. (Eggnog will thicken as it cools.) Stir in bourbon just before serving. **Yield: 5 cups.**

*For testing purposes only, we used Woodford Reserve Bourbon.

metric equivalents

The recipes that appear in this cookbook use the standard U.S. method for measuring liquid and dry or solid ingredients (teaspoons, tablespoons, and cups). The information in the following charts is provided to help cooks outside the United States successfully use these recipes. All equivalents are approximate.

Metric Equivalents for Different Types of Ingredients

A standard cup measure of a dry or solid ingredient will vary in weight depending on the type of ingredient. A standard cup of liquid is the same volume for any type of liquid. Use the following chart when converting standard cup measures to grams (weight) or milliliters (volume).

Standard Cup	Fine Powder (ex. flour)	Grain (ex. rice)	Granular (ex. sugar)	Liquid Solids (ex. butter)	Liquid (ex. milk)
1	140 g	150 g	190 g	200 g	240 ml
¾	105 g	113 g	143 g	150 g	180 ml
⅔	93 g	100 g	125 g	133 g	160 ml
½	70 g	75 g	95 g	100 g	120 ml
⅓	47 g	50 g	63 g	67 g	80 ml
¼	35 g	38 g	48 g	50 g	60 ml
⅛	18 g	19 g	24 g	25 g	30 ml

Useful Equivalents for Dry Ingredients by Weight

(To convert ounces to grams, multiply the number of ounces by 30.)

1 oz	=	¹⁄₁₆ lb	=	30 g
4 oz	=	¼ lb	=	120 g
8 oz	=	½ lb	=	240 g
12 oz	=	¾ lb	=	360 g
16 oz	=	1 lb	=	480 g

Useful Equivalents for Length

(To convert inches to centimeters, multiply the number of inches by 2.5.)

1 in				=	2.5 cm		
6 in	=	½ ft		=	15 cm		
12 in	=	1 ft		=	30 cm		
36 in	=	3 ft	=	1 yd	=	90 cm	
40 in				=	100 cm	=	1 m

Useful Equivalents for Liquid Ingredients by Volume

¼ tsp						=	1 ml	
½ tsp						=	2 ml	
1 tsp						=	5 ml	
3 tsp	=	1 Tbsp			= ½ fl oz	=	15 ml	
		2 Tbsp	=	⅛ cup	= 1 fl oz	=	30 ml	
		4 Tbsp	=	¼ cup	= 2 fl oz	=	60 ml	
		5⅓ Tbsp	=	⅓ cup	= 3 fl oz	=	80 ml	
		8 Tbsp	=	½ cup	= 4 fl oz	=	120 ml	
		10⅔ Tbsp	=	⅔ cup	= 5 fl oz	=	160 ml	
		12 Tbsp	=	¾ cup	= 6 fl oz	=	180 ml	
		16 Tbsp	=	1 cup	= 8 fl oz	=	240 ml	
		1 pt	=	2 cups	= 16 fl oz	=	480 ml	
		1 qt	=	4 cups	= 32 fl oz	=	960 ml	
					33 fl oz	=	1000 ml	= 1 l

Useful Equivalents for Cooking/Oven Temperatures

	Fahrenheit	Celsius	Gas Mark
Freeze water	32° F	0° C	
Room temperature	68° F	20° C	
Boil water	212° F	100° C	
Bake	325° F	160° C	3
	350° F	180° C	4
	375° F	190° C	5
	400° F	200° C	6
	425° F	220° C	7
	450° F	230° C	8
Broil			Grill

{ index }

Essays

For my birthday, my mother always made me my favorite dessert and the only true comfort of my childhood, pumpkin pie. Every October 26, she made a pumpkin pie and decorated it with candles. I watched as she rolled out the pie crust with ease and good humor, and it always turned out golden and luscious. Once I tried to make a pumpkin pie from scratch and ended up with a product that was ghastly, inedible, and painful to the human spirit. I had killed a good pumpkin for no good reason. I learned to always use canned pumpkin for your pies—those people know what they are doing. I can't think about pumpkin pie now without smiling and thinking of my pretty mother. This is her recipe, and I am writing it on my birthday.

—Pat Conroy

Pumpkin Pie

2   eggs
1   (15-ounce) can pumpkin (not filling)
½   cup sugar
1   teaspoon ground cinnamon
¼   teaspoon ground cloves
Pinch salt
1   (12-ounce) can evaporated milk
1   (10-inch) prepared, unbaked pie crust

Beat eggs in a mixing bowl; add pumpkin, sugar, spices, and salt. Add milk, stirring well. Pour into pie shell. Bake at 425° for 15 minutes; then reduce heat to 350° and bake an additional 40 minutes or until filling is set and browned. **Yield: 6 to 8 servings.**